# HOW TO READ A PAPER
The basics of evidence based medicine

TRISHA GREENHALGH
Senior Lecturer
Unit for Evidence-Based Practice and Policy
Joint Department of Primary Care
and Population Sciences
University College London Medical School
and Royal Free Hospital School of Medicine
Whittington Hospital, London, UK

BMJ
Publishing
Group

© BMJ Publishing Group 1997

First published in 1997
Second impression 1997
Third impression 1998
Fourth impression 1998
by the BMJ Publishing Group, BMA House, Tavistock Square,
London WC1H 9JR

**British Library Cataloguing in Publication Data**

A catalogue record for this book is available from the British Library

ISBN 0-7279-1139-2

Typeset and printed by Derry, Nottingham

# HOW TO READ A PAPER

# Contents

In November 1995, Ruth Holland, book reviews editor of the *British Medical Journal*, suggested that I write a book to demystify the important but often inaccessible subject of evidence based medicine. She provided invaluable comments on earlier drafts of the manuscript but was tragically killed in a train crash on 8th August 1996. This book is dedicated to her memory.

# Foreword

Not surprisingly, the wide publicity given to what is now called "evidence based medicine" has been greeted with mixed reactions by those who are involved in the provision of patient care. The bulk of the medical profession seems to be slightly hurt by the concept, suggesting as it does that until recently all medical practice was what Lewis Thomas has described as a frivolous and irresponsible kind of human experimentation, based on nothing but trial and error, and usually resulting in precisely that sequence. On the other hand, politicians and those who administrate our health services have greeted the notion with enormous glee. They had suspected all along that doctors were totally uncritical and now they had it on paper. Evidence based medicine came as a gift from the gods because, at least as they perceived it, its implied efficiency must inevitably result in cost saving.

The concept of controlled clinical trials and evidence based medicine is not, however, new. It is recorded that Frederick II, Emperor of the Romans and King of Sicily and Jerusalem, who lived from 1192 to 1250 AD, and who was interested in the effects of exercise on the digestion, took two knights and gave them identical meals. One was then sent out hunting and the other ordered to bed. At the end of several hours he killed both and examined the contents of their ailmentary canals; digestion had proceeded further in the stomach of the sleeping knight. In the 17th century Jan Baptista van Helmont, a physician and philosopher, became sceptical of the practice of blood letting. Hence he proposed what was almost certainly the first clinical trial involving large numbers, randomisation, and statistical analysis. This entailed taking 200 to 500 poor people, dividing them into two groups by casting lots, and protecting one from phlebotomy while allowing the other to be treated with as much blood letting as his colleagues thought appropriate. The number of funerals in each group would be used to assess the efficacy of blood letting. History does not record why this splendid experiment was never carried out.

If modern scientific medicine can be said to have had a beginning it was in Paris in the mid-19th century and where it had its roots in the work and teachings of Pierre Charles Alexandre Louis. Louis introduced statistical analysis to the evaluation of medical treatment and, incidentally, showed that blood letting was a valueless form of treatment, though this did not change the habits of the physicians of the time or for many years to come. Despite this pioneering work few clinicians on either side of the Atlantic urged that trials of clinical outcome should be adopted, although the principles of numerically based experimental design were enunciated in the 1920s by the geneticist Ronald Fisher. The field started to make a major impact on clinical practice only after the second world war after the seminal work of Sir Austin Bradford Hill and the British epidemiologists who followed him, notably Richard Doll and Archie Cochrane.

But although the idea of evidence based medicine is not new, modern disciples like David Sackett and his colleagues are doing a great service to clinical practice, not just by popularising the idea but by bringing home to clinicians the notion that it is not a dry academic subject but more a way of thinking that should permeate every aspect of medical practice. While much of it is based on megatrials and meta-analyses, it should also be used to influence almost everything that a doctor does. After all, the medical profession has been brain washed for years by examiners in medical schools and Royal Colleges to believe that there is only one way of examining a patient. Our bedside rituals could do with as much critical evaluation as our operations and drug regimens; the same goes for almost every aspect of doctoring.

As clinical practice becomes busier and time for reading and reflection becomes even more precious the ability to peruse the medical literature effectively and, in the future, to become familiar with a knowledge of best practice from modern communication systems, will be essential skills for doctors. In this lively book Trisha Greenhalgh provides an excellent approach to how to make best use of medical literature and the benefits of evidence based medicine. It should have equal appeal for first year medical students and grey haired consultants and deserves to be read widely.

With increasing years the privilege of being invited to write a foreword to a book by one's former students becomes less of a rarity. Trisha Greenhalgh was the kind of medical student who never let her teachers get away with a loose thought, and this inquiring attitude seems to have flowered over the years; this is a splendid and timely book and I wish it all the success it deserves. After all, the concept of evidence based medicine is nothing more than the state of mind that every clinical teacher hopes to develop in their students; Dr Greenhalgh's sceptical but constructive approach to medical literature suggests that such a happy outcome is possible at least once in the lifetime of a professor of medicine.

David Weatherall

# Preface: Do you need to read this book?

This book is intended for anyone, whether medically qualified or not, who wants to find their way into the medical literature, assess the scientific validity and practical relevance of the articles they find, and, when appropriate, put the results into practice. These skills constitute the basics of evidence based medicine.

I hope it will help you to read and interpret medical papers better. I hope, in addition, to convey a further message, which is this. Many of the descriptions given by cynics of what evidence based medicine is (the glorification of things that can be measured without regard for the usefulness or accuracy of what is measured, the uncritical acceptance of published numerical data, the preparation of all encompassing guidelines by self appointed "experts" who are out of touch with real medicine, the debasement of clinical freedom through the imposition of rigid and dogmatic clinical protocols, and the over-reliance on simplistic, inappropriate, and often incorrect economic analyses) are actually criticisms of what the evidence based medicine movement is fighting *against,* rather than of what it represents.

Do not, however, think of me as an evangelist for the gospel according to evidence based medicine. I believe that the science of finding, evaluating, and implementing the results of medical research can, and often does, make patient care more objective, more logical, and more cost effective. If I didn't believe that, I wouldn't spend so much of my time teaching it and trying, as a general practitioner, to practise it. Nevertheless, I believe that when it is applied in a vacuum (that is, in the absence of common sense and without regard to the individual circumstances and priorities of the person being offered treatment) the evidence based approach to patient care is a reductionist process with a real potential for harm.

Finally, you should note that I am neither an epidemiologist nor a statistician but a person who reads papers and who has developed a pragmatic (and at times unconventional) system for testing their merits. If you want to pursue the epidemiological or statistical themes covered, I would encourage you to move on to more definitive texts, references for which you will find at the end of each chapter.

Trisha Greenhalgh

# Acknowledgements

I am not by any standards an expert on all of the subjects covered here (in particular, I am very bad at sums), and I am grateful to the people listed below for help along the way. I am, however, the final author of every chapter, and responsibility for any inaccuracies is mine alone. I thank:

PROFESSOR DAVE SACKETT and PROFESSOR ANDY HAINES—for inspiration and encouragement.

The following medical information experts (previously known as librarians), for vital input into chapter 2 and the appendices on search strings: MR REINHARDT WENTZ of Charing Cross and Westminster Medical School, London; MS JANE ROWLANDS of the BMA library in London; MS CAROL LEFEBVRE of the UK Cochrane Centre, Oxford; and MS VALERIE WILDRIDGE of the Kings's Fund library in London. I strongly recommend Jane Rowlands' Introductory and Advanced Medline courses at the BMA library.

The following expert advisers and proofreaders: DR SARAH WALTERS and DR JONATHAN ELFORD (chapters 3, 4, and 7), DR ANDREW HERXHEIMER (chapter 6), PROFESSOR IAIN CHALMERS (chapter 8), DR BRIAN HURWITZ (chapter 9), PROFESSOR MIKE DRUMMOND and DR ALISON TONKS (chapter 10), PROFESSOR NICK BLACK and DR ROD TAYLOR (chapter 11), and DR JOHN DOBBY (chapters 5 and 12).

MR NICK MOLE, of Ovid Technologies Ltd, for checking chapter 2 and providing demonstration software for me to play with.

Thanks also to my family for sparing me the time and space to finish this book.

# Chapter 1: Why read papers at all?

## 1.1 Does "evidence based medicine" simply mean "reading medical papers"?

Evidence based medicine is much more than just reading papers. According to one definition it is "the conscientious, explicit, and judicious use of current best evidence in making decisions about the care of individual patients"[1]. If you follow this approach, all sorts of issues relating to your patients (or, if you work in public health medicine, planning or purchasing issues relating to groups of patients or patient populations) will prompt you to ask questions about scientific evidence, seek answ     to those questions in a systematic way, and alter your pr     tice accordingly.

You might ask questions, for example, about a patient's symptoms ("In a 34 year old man with left sided chest pain, what is the probability that there is a serious heart problem, and if there is, will it show up on a resting ECG?"), about physical or diagnostic signs ("In an otherwise uncomplicated childbirth, does the presence of meconium (indicating fetal bowel movement) in the amniotic fluid indicate considerable deterioration in the physiological state of the fetus?"), about the prognosis of an illness ("If a previously well 2 year old has a short fit associated with a high temperature, what is the chance that she will subsequently develop epilepsy?"), about treatment ("In patients with an acute myocardial infarction (heart attack) are the risks associated with thrombolytic drugs (clotbusters) outweighed by the benefits, whatever the patient's age, sex, and ethnic origin?"), about cost-effectiveness ("To reduce the suicide rate in a health district, is it better to employ more consultant psychiatrists, more community psychiatric nurses, or more counsellors?"), and about a host of other aspects of health and health services.

Professor Dave Sackett, in the opening editorial of the very first issue of the journal *Evidence Based Medicine* summarises the essential steps in the emerging science of evidence based medicine[2]:

- To convert our information needs into answerable questions (that is, to formulate the problem)

- To track down, with maximum efficiency, the best evidence with which to answer these questions—which may come from the clinical examination, the diagnostic laboratory, the published literature, or other sources

- To appraise the evidence critically (that is, weigh it up) to assess its validity (closeness to the truth) and usefulness (clinical applicability)

- To implement the results of this appraisal in our clinical practice

- To evaluate our performance.

Hence, evidence based medicine requires you not only to read papers but to read the *right* papers at the right time and then to alter your behaviour (and, what is often more difficult, the behaviour of other people) in the light of what you have found. I am concerned that the plethora of how-to-do-it courses in evidence based medicine so often concentrate on the third of these five steps (critical appraisal) to the exclusion of all the others. Yet if you have asked the wrong question or sought answers from the wrong sources, you might as well not read any papers at all. Equally, all your training in search techniques and critical appraisal will go to waste if you do not put at least as much effort into implementing valid evidence and measuring progress towards your goals as you do into reading the paper.

If I were to be pedantic about the title of this book, these broader aspects of evidence based medicine should not even get a mention here. But I hope you would have demanded your money back if I had omitted the final section of this chapter (Before you start: formulate the problem), chapter 2 (Searching the literature), and chapter 12 (Implementing evidence based practice). Chapters 3 to 11 describe step three of the evidence based medicine process: critical appraisal—that is, what you should do when you actually have the paper in front of you.

Incidentally, if you are computer literate and want to explore the subject of evidence based medicine on the Internet, you could try the following web sites: (http://www.shef.ac.uk/uni/academic/R-Z/scharr/ir/netting.html (SCHARR); http://cebm.jr2.ox.ac.uk (Oxford Centre for Evidenced Based Medicine); http://www.ucl.ac.uk/primcare-popsci/uebpp/uebpp.htm (my own website)). If you're not, don't worry.

## 1.2 Why do people often groan when you mention evidence based medicine?

Critics of evidence based medicine might define it as "the increasingly fashionable tendency of a group of young, confident, and highly numerate medical academics to belittle the performance of experienced clinicians by using a combination of epidemiological jargon and statistical sleight-of-hand", or "the argument, usually presented with near evangelistic zeal, that no health related action should ever be taken by a doctor, a nurse, a purchaser of health services, or a politician unless and until the results of several large and expensive research trials have appeared in print and approved by a committee of experts".

Others have put their reservations even more strongly: "evidence based medicine seems to [replace] original findings with subjectively selected, arbitrarily summarised, laundered and biased conclusions of indeterminate validity or completeness. It has been carried out by people of unknown ability, experience, and skills using methods whose opacity prevents assessment of the original data"[3].

The palpable resentment among many health professionals towards the evidence based medicine movement is mostly a reaction to the implication that doctors (and nurses, midwives, physiotherapists and other health professionals) were functionally illiterate until they were shown the light and that the few who weren't illiterate wilfully ignored published medical evidence. Anyone who works face to face with patients knows how often it is necessary to seek new information before making a clinical

3

decision. Doctors have spent time in libraries since libraries were invented. We don't put a patient on a new drug without evidence that it is likely to work—apart from anything else, such off-licence use of medication is, strictly speaking, illegal. Surely we have all been practising evidence based medicine for years, except when we were deliberately bluffing (using the "placebo" effect for good medical reasons) or when we were ill, overstressed, or consciously being lazy?

Well, no, we haven't. There have been several surveys on the behaviour of doctors, nurses, and related professionals[4–7], and most of them reached the same conclusion: clinical decisions are only rarely based on the best available evidence. Estimates in the early 1980s suggested that only around 10-20% of medical interventions (drug therapies, surgical operations, $x$ rays, blood tests, and so on) were based on sound scientific evidence[8 9]. These figures have since been disputed as they were derived by assessing all diagnostic and therapeutic procedures currently in use, so that each procedure, however obscure, carried equal weight in the final fraction. A more recent evaluation with this method classified 21% of health technologies as evidence based[10].

Surveys that look at the interventions chosen for consecutive series of patients, which reflect the technologies that are actually used rather than simply those that are on the market, have suggested that 60-90% of clinical decisions, dependent on the speciality, are "evidence based"[11–13]. But as I have argued elsewhere[14], these studies had methodological limitations. Apart from anything else, they were undertaken in specialised units and looked at the practice of world experts in evidence based medicine; hence, the figures arrived at can hardly be generalised beyond their immediate setting (see section 4.2).

Let's take a look at the various approaches that health professionals use to reach their decisions in reality—all of which are examples of what evidence based medicine *isn't*.

### Decision making by anecdote

When I was a medical student, I occasionally joined the retinue of a distinguished professor as he made his daily ward rounds. On seeing a new patient, he would inquire about the patient's symptoms, turn to the massed ranks of juniors around the bed, and relate the story of a similar patient encountered 20 to 30 years previously. "Ah, yes. I remember we gave her such-and-such, and she was fine after that". He was cynical, often rightly, about new drugs and technologies, and his clinical acumen was second to none. Nevertheless, it had taken him 40 years to accumulate his expertise, and the largest medical textbook of all—the collection of cases that were outside his personal experience—was forever closed to him.

The dangers of decision making by anecdote are well illustrated by considering the risk-benefit ratio of drugs and medicines. In my first pregnancy, I developed severe vomiting and was given the antisickness drug prochlorperazine. Within minutes, I went into an uncontrollable and very distressing neurological spasm. Two days later, I had recovered fully from this idiosyncratic reaction, but I have never prescribed the drug since, even though the estimated prevalence of serious neurological reactions to prochlorperazine is only one in several thousand cases. Conversely, it is tempting to dismiss the possibility of rare but potentially serious adverse effects from familiar drugs; such as thrombosis on the contraceptive pill, when one has never encountered such problems in oneself or one's patients.

We clinicians would not be human if we ignored our personal clinical experiences, but we would be better to base our decisions on the collective experience of thousands of clinicians treating millions of patients, rather than on what we as individuals have seen and felt. Chapter 5 (Statistics for the non-statistician) describes some more objective methods, such as the number needed to treat (NNT), for deciding whether a particular drug (or other intervention) is likely to do a patient considerable good or harm.

*Decision making by press cutting*

For the first 10 years after I qualified, I kept an expanding file of papers that I had ripped out of my medical weeklies before binning the less interesting parts. If an article or editorial seemed to have something new to say, I consciously altered my clinical practice in line with its conclusions. All children with suspected urinary tract infections should be sent for scans of the kidneys to exclude congenital abnormalities, said one article, so I began referring anyone under the age of 16 with urinary symptoms for specialist investigations. The advice was in print and it was recent so it must surely replace traditional practice—in this case, referring only children below the age of 10 who had had two well documented infections.

This approach to clinical decision making is still very common. How many doctors do you know who justify their approach to a particular clinical problem by citing the results section of a single published study, even though they could not tell you anything at all about the methods used to obtain those results? Was the trial randomised and controlled (see section 3.3)? How many patients, of what age, sex and disease severity, were involved (see section 4.2)? How many "dropped out" of the study and why (see section 4.6)? By what criteria were patients judged cured? If the findings of the study seemed to contradict those of other researchers, what attempt was made to validate (confirm) and replicate (repeat) them (see section 8.3)? Were the statistical tests that allegedly proved the authors' point appropriately chosen and correctly performed (see chapter 5)? Doctors (and nurses, midwives, medical managers, psychologists, medical students, and consumer activists) who like to cite the results of medical research studies have a responsibility to ensure that they first go through a checklist of questions like these (more of which are listed in appendix A).

### Decision making by expert opinion

An important variant of decision making by press cutting is the use of "off the peg" reviews, editorials, consensus statements, and guidelines. The medical freebies (free medical journals and other "information sheets", usually sponsored directly or indirectly by the pharmaceutical industry) are replete with potted recommendations and at a glance management guides. But who says the advice given in a set of guidelines, a punchy editorial, or an amply referenced "overview" is correct?

Professor Cynthia Mulrow, one of the founders of the science of systematic review (see chapter 8) has shown that experts in a particular clinical speciality are actually *less* likely to provide an objective review of all the available evidence than a non-expert who approaches the literature with unbiased eyes[15]. In extreme cases, an "expert review" may consist simply of the lifelong bad habits and personal press cuttings of an aging clinician. Chapter 8 takes you through a checklist for assessing whether a "systematic review" written by someone else really merits the description, and chapter 9 discusses the potential limitations of off the peg clinical guidelines.

*Decision making by cost minimisation*

The general public is usually horrified when it learns that a treatment has been withheld from a patient for reasons of cost. Managers, politicians, and, increasingly, doctors, can count on being pilloried by the press when a child with a brain tumour is not sent to a specialist unit in America or a frail old lady is denied indefinite board and lodging on an acute medical ward. Yet in the real world, all health care is provided from a limited budget, and it is increasingly recognised that clinical decisions must take into account the economic costs of a given intervention. As chapter 10 argues, clinical decision making *purely* on the grounds of cost ("cost minimisation"—purchasing the cheapest option with no regard to how effective it is) is usually both senseless and cruel, and we are right to object vocally when this occurs.

Expensive interventions should not, however, be justified simply because they are new or because they ought to work in theory or because the only alternative is to do nothing—but because they are very likely to save life or considerably improve its quality. How, though, can the benefits of a hip replacement in a 75 year old be meaningfully compared with that of cholesterol lowering drugs in a middle aged man or infertility investigations for a couple in their 20s? Somewhat counter intuitively, there is no self evident set of ethical principles or analytical tools that we can use to match limited resources to unlimited demand. As you will see in chapter 10, the much derided quality adjusted life year (QALY) and similar utility based units are simply attempts to lend some objectivity to the illogical but unavoidable comparison of apples with oranges in the field of human suffering.

There is another reason why people find the term evidence based medicine unpalatable. This chapter has argued that evidence based medicine is about coping with change, not about knowing all the answers before you start. In other words, it is not so much about what you have read in the past but about how you go about identifying and meeting your ongoing learning needs and applying your knowledge appropriately and consistently in new clinical settings. Doctors who were brought up in the old school style of never admitting ignorance may find it hard to accept that some aspect of scientific uncertainty is encountered, on average, three times for every two patients seen by experienced teaching hospital consultants[16] (and, no doubt, even more often by their less up to date provincial colleagues). An evidence based approach to ward

7

rounds may turn the traditional medical hierarchy on its head when the staff nurse or junior doctor produces new evidence that challenges what the consultant taught everyone last week. For some senior clinicians, learning the skills of critical appraisal is the least of their problems in adjusting to an evidence based teaching style.

## 1.3 Before you start: formulate the problem

When I ask my medical students to write me an essay about high blood pressure, they often produce long, scholarly, and essentially correct statements on what high blood pressure is, what causes it, and what the treatment options are. On the day they hand their essays in, most of them know far more about high blood pressure than I do. They are certainly aware that high blood pressure is the single most common cause of stroke and that detecting and treating everyone's high blood pressure would cut the incidence of stroke by almost half. Most of them are aware that stroke, though devastating when it happens, is a fairly rare event, and that blood pressure tablets have side effects such as tiredness, dizziness, impotence, and getting "caught short" when a long way from the lavatory.

But when I ask my students a practical question such as "Mrs Jones has developed light headedness on these blood pressure tablets and she wants to stop all medication; what would you advise her to do?", they are foxed. They sympathise with Mrs Jones' predicament, but they cannot distil from their pages of close-written text the one thing that Mrs Jones needs to know. As Richard Smith (paraphrasing TS Eliot) asked recently in a *BMJ* editorial: "Where is the wisdom we have lost in knowledge, and the knowledge we have lost in information?"[17].

Experienced doctors (and many nurses) might think they can answer Mrs Jones' question from their own personal experience. As I argued earlier in this chapter, few of them would be right[4]. And even if they were right on this occasion, they would still need an overall system for converting the rag-bag of information about a patient (an ill defined set of symptoms, physical signs, test results, and knowledge of what happened to this patient or a similar patient last time), the particular anxieties and values (utilities) of the patient, and other things that could be relevant (a hunch, a half remembered article, the opinion of an older and wiser colleague, or a paragraph discovered by chance while flicking through a textbook) into a succinct summary of what the problem is and what specific additional items of information we need to solve that problem.

Sackett and colleagues have recently helped us by dissecting the parts of a good clinical question[18].

- First, define precisely *who* the question is about (that is, ask "How would I describe a group of patients similar to this one?")

- Next, define *which* manoeuvre you are considering in this patient or population (for example, a drug treatment) and, if necessary, a comparison manoeuvre (for example, placebo or current standard therapy)

- Finally, define the desired (or undesired) *outcome* (for example, reduced mortality, better quality of life, overall cost savings to the health service, and so on).

The second step may not, in fact, concern a drug treatment, surgical operation, or other intervention. The "manoeuvre" could, for example, be the exposure to a putative carcinogen (something that might cause cancer) or the detection of a particular surrogate end point in a blood test or other investigation. (A surrogate end point, as Section 6.3 explains, is something that predicts, or is said to predict, the later development or progression of disease. In reality, there are few tests that reliably act as crystal balls for patients' medical future. The statement "The doctor looked at the test results and told me I had six months to live" usually reflects either poor memory or irresponsible doctoring!) In both these cases, the "outcome" would be the development of cancer (or some other disease) several years later. In most clinical problems with individual patients, however, the "manoeuvre" consists of a specific intervention initiated by a health professional.

Thus, in Mrs Jones's case, we might ask, "In a 68 year old white woman with essential (that is, common or garden) hypertension (high blood pressure), no coexisting illness, and no relevant medical history, do the benefits of continuing treatment with hydrochlorthiazide (chiefly, reduced risk of stroke) outweigh the inconvenience?" Note that in framing the specific question, we have already established that Mrs Jones has never had a heart attack, stroke, or early warning signs such as transient paralysis or

9

loss of vision. If she had, her risk of subsequent stroke would be much higher and we would, rightly, load the risk-benefit equation to reflect this.

To answer the question we have posed we must determine not just the risk of stroke in untreated hypertension but also the likely reduction in that risk that we can expect with drug treatment. This is, in fact, a rephrasing of a more general question (do the benefits of treatment in this case outweigh the risks?) that we should have asked before we prescribed hydrochlorthiazide to Mrs Jones in the first place and that all doctors should, of course, ask themselves every time they reach for their prescription pad.

Remember that Mrs Jones's alternative to staying on this particular drug is not necessarily to take no drugs at all; there may be other drugs with equivalent efficacy but less disabling side effects (remember that, as chapter 6 argues, too many clinical trials of new drugs compare the product with placebo rather than with the best available alternative) or non-medical treatments such as exercise, salt restriction, homeopathy, or acupuncture. Not all of these approaches would help Mrs Jones or be acceptable to her, but it would be quite appropriate to seek evidence as to *whether* they might help her.

We will probably find answers to some of these questions in the medical literature, and chapter 2 describes how to search for relevant papers once you have formulated the problem. But before you start, give one last thought to your patient with high blood pressure. To determine her personal priorities (how does she value a 10% reduction in her risk of stroke in five years' time compared with the inability to go shopping unaccompanied today?), you will need to approach Mrs Jones, not a blood pressure specialist or the Medline database. The patient's perspective can be formally integrated into the evidence based medicine approach by using a decision tree model[19][20], but in practice this rarely happens, and the patient's own perspective on their illness may be dismissed in favour of a column of QALYs calculated by a medical statistician. This and other absurdities that can result from an unthinking acceptance of a narrow evidence based medicine paradigm have been considered in detail by its critics[21]. It should be noted, however, that the evidence based medicine movement is making rapid progress in developing a more practical methodology for incorporating the patient's perspective in both clinical decision making[14][22] and the design and conduct of research trials[23]. I have attempted to incorporate the patient's perspective into Sackett's five stage model for evidence based practice[1]; the resulting eight stages, which I have called a context sensitive checklist for evidence based practice, are shown in appendix A.

## Exercise 1

1  Go back to the second paragraph in this chapter, where examples of clinical questions are given. Decide whether each of these is a properly focused question in terms of:

- The patient or problem

- The manoeuvre (intervention, prognostic marker, exposure)

- The comparison manoeuvre, if appropriate

- The clinical outcome.

2  Now try the following:

a) A 5 year old child has been on high dose topical steroids for severe eczema since the age of 20 months. The mother believes that the steroids are stunting the child's growth and wants to change to homeopathic treatment. What information does the dermatologist need to decide a) whether she is right about the topical steroids and b) whether homeopathic treatment will help this child?

b) A woman who is nine weeks pregnant calls out her GP because of abdominal pain and bleeding. A previous ultrasound scan has confirmed that the pregnancy is not ectopic. The GP decides that she might be having a miscarriage and tells her she must go into hospital for a scan and, possibly, an operation to clear out the womb. The woman refuses. What information do they both need to establish whether hospital admission is medically necessary?

c) In the UK, most parents take their babies at the age of 6 weeks, 8 months, 18 months, and 3 years for developmental checks, where a doctor listens for heart murmurs, feels the abdomen, and checks that the testicles are present and a nurse shakes a rattle and counts how many bricks the infant can build into a tower. Ignoring the social aspects of "well baby clinics", what information would you need to decide whether the service is a good use of health resources?

1 Sackett DL, Rosenberg WMC, Gray JAM, *et al,* Evidence based medicine: what it is and what it isn't. *BMJ* 1996; **312**: 71-2.

2 Sackett DL, Haynes B. On the need for evidence-based medicine. *Evidence-Based Medicine* 1995; **1**: 4-5.

3 James NT. Scientific method and raw data should be considered (letter). *BMJ* 1996; **313**: 169-70.

4 Institute of Medicine. *Guidelines for clinical practice: from development to use.* Washington, DC: National Academy Press, 1992.

5 Brook RH, Williams KN, Avery SB. Quality assurance today and tomorrow: forecast for the future. *Ann Intern Med* 1976; **85**: 809-17.

6 Roper WL, Winkenwerde W, Hackbarth GM, *et al.* Effectiveness in health care: an initiative to evaluate and improve medical practice. *N Engl J Med* 1988; **319**: 1197-202.

7 Sackett DL, Haynes RB, Guyatt GH, *et al. Clinical epidemiology—a basic science for clinical medicine.* London; Little, Brown, 1991: 305-33.

8 Office of Technology Assessment of the Congress of the United States. *The impact of randomised clinical trials on health policy and medical practice.* Washington DC: US Government Printing Office, 1983.

9 Williamson JW. Goldschmidt PG, Jillson IA. *Medical practice information demonstration project: final report.* Baltimore, Maryland: Policy Research, 1979.

10 Dubinsky M, Ferguson JH. Analysis of the National Institutes of Health Medicare Coverage Assessment. *Int J Technol Assess Health Care* 1990; **6**: 480-8.

11 Ellis J, Mulligan I, Rowe J, Sackett DL. Inpatient general medicine is evidence-based. A-team, Nuffield Department of Clinical Medicine. *Lancet* 1995; **346**: 407-10.

12 Gill P, Dowell AC, Neal RD, *et al.* Evidence based general practice: a retrospective study of interventions in one training practice. *BMJ* 1996; **312**: 819-21.

13 Geddes J, Game D, Jenkins N, *et al.* What proportion of primary psychiatric interventions are based on evidence from randomised controlled trials. *Quality in Health Care* 1996; **(4)**: 215-7.

14 Greenhalgh T. Is my practice evidence-based? (editorial). *BMJ* 1996; **313**: 957-8.

15 Mulrow C. Rationale for systematic reviews. *BMJ* 1994; **309**: 597-9.

16 Covell DG, Uman GC, Manning PR. Information needs in office practice: Are they being met? *Ann Intern Med* 1985; **103**: 596-9.

17 Smith R. Where is the wisdom...? *BMJ* 1991; **303**: 798-9.

18 Sackett DL, Richardson WS, Rosenberg WMC, Haynes RB. *Evidence-based medicine: how to practice and teach ebm.* London; Churchill-Livingstone, 1996.

19 Kassirer JP. Incorporating patients' preferences into medical decisions. *N Engl J Med* 1994; **330**: 1895-6.

20 Dowie J. 'Evidence-based', 'cost-effective', and 'preference-driven' medicine. *J Health Serv Res Policy* 1996; **1**: 104-13.

21 Grimley Evans, J. Evidence-based and evidence-biased medicine. *Age Ageing* 1995; **24**: 461-3.

22 Greenhalgh T, Young G. Applying the evidence with patients. In: Silagy C, Haines AP, eds. *Evidence-based medicine in primary care.* London: BMJ Books 1998 (in press).

23 Fulford KWM, Ersser S, Hope T. *Essential practice in patient-centred care.* Oxford; Blackwell Science, 1996.

# Chapter 2
# Searching the literature

## 2.1 Reading medical articles

Navigating one's way through the jungle that calls itself the medical literature is no easy task, and I make no apology that this chapter is the longest in the book. You can apply all the rules for reading a paper correctly but if you're reading the wrong paper you might as well be doing something else entirely. There are already over 10 million medical articles on our library shelves. Every month, around 4000 medical journals are published worldwide, and the number of different journals that now exist solely to summarise the articles in the remainder probably exceeds 200. Only 10-15% of the material that appears in print today will subsequently prove to be of lasting scientific value.

Dr David Jewell, writing in the excellent book, *Critical Reading for Primary Care*, reminds us that there are three levels of reading[1]:

● *browsing*—in which we flick through books and journals looking for anything that might interest us

● *reading for information*—in which we approach the literature looking for answers to a specific question, usually related to a problem we have met in real life

● *reading for research*—in which we seek to gain a comprehensive view of the existing state of knowledge, ignorance, and uncertainty in a defined topic.

In practice, most of us get most of our information (and, let's face it, a good deal of pleasure) from browsing. To overapply the rules for critical appraisal that follow in the rest of this book would be to kill the enjoyment of casual reading. Jewell warns us, however, to steer a careful path between the bland gullibility of believing everything and the strenuous intellectualism of formal critical appraisal.

## 2.2 The Medline database

If you are browsing (reading for the fun of it) you can read what you like, in whatever order you wish. If reading for information (focused searching) or research (systematic review) you will waste time and miss many valuable articles if you simply search at random. Many (but not all, see section 2.10) medical articles are indexed in the huge Medline database, access to which is almost universal in medical and science libraries in developed countries.

Medline is compiled by the National Library of Medicine of the United States and indexes over 3800 journals published in over 70 countries. Three versions of the information in Medline are available:

- Printed (the *Index Medicus*, a manual index updated every year, from which the electronic version is compiled)

- On line (the whole database from 1966 to date on a mainframe computer, accessed over the Internet or other electronic server)

- CD ROM (the whole database on between 10 and 18 CDs, depending on who makes it).

The Medline database is exactly the same, whichever company is selling it, but the commands you need to type in to access it differ according to the CD ROM software. Commercial vendors of Medline on line and/or on CD ROM include Ovid Technologies (OVID), Silver Platter Information Ltd (WinSPIRS), EBSCO, and Knight-Ridder.

The best way to learn to use Medline is to book a session with a trained librarian or other experienced user. Unless you are a technophobe, you can pick up the basics in less than an hour. Remember that articles can be traced in two ways:

- By any word listed on the database, including words in the title, abstract, authors' names, and the institution where the research was done (note—the *abstract* is a short summary of what the article is all about that you will find on the database as well as at the beginning of the printed article)

- By a restricted thesaurus of medical titles, known as medical subject heading (MeSH) terms.

To illustrate how Medline works, I have worked through some common problems in searching. The following scenarios have been drawn up with OVID software (because that's what I and most people use and because it is the version used by the dial-up service of the BMA library, to which all BMA members with a modem have free access). The practical exercises included in this chapter are all equally possible with the other search software.

## 2.3 Problem 1—You are trying to find a particular paper that you know exists

*Solution—Search the database by field suffix (title, author, journal, institution, etc) or by textwords*

This shouldn't take long. You do not need to do a comprehensive subject search. Get into the part of the database that covers the approximate year of the paper's publication (usually the past five years). Selecting this is one of the first things the system asks you to do on the main Medline search screen; if you're already in the main Medline menu, select "database" (Alt-B).

If you know the title of the paper (or the approximate title) and perhaps the journal in which it was published, you can use the title and journal search keys *or* (this is quicker) the **.ti** and **.jn** field suffixes. (Note—on previous versions of OVID, the syntax for field suffixes included a full stop after the letters; the latest version does not require this). Box 2.1 shows some useful field suffixes, most of which are self explanatory. But note the **.ui** suffix, which denotes the unique number that you can use to identify a particular Medline entry. If you find an article that you might want to call up again, it's often quicker to write down the unique identifier rather than the author, title, journal, and so on.

---

### Box 2.1 Useful search field suffixes (OVID)

| Syntax | Meaning | Example |
|--------|---------|---------|
| .ab | Word in abstract | **epilepsy.ab** |
| .au | Author | **smith-r.au** |
| .jn | Journal | **lancet.jn** |
| .me | Single word, wherever it may appear as a MeSH term | **ulcer.me** |
| .ti | Word in title | **epilepsy.ti** |
| .tw | Word in title or abstract | **epilepsy.tw** |
| .ui | Unique identifier | **91574637.ui** |
| .yr | Year of publication | **97.yr** |

---

15

To illustrate the use of field suffixes, let's say you are trying to find a paper called something like "Confidentiality and patients' casenotes", which you remember seeing in the *British Journal of General Practice* a couple of years ago. Type the following into the computer:

**1        confidentiality.ti**

This gives you about 250 possible articles in set 1. Now type:

**2        british journal of general practice.jn**

This gives you about 900 articles in set 2—that is, all articles listed in this part of the Medline database for the years you selected from the *British Journal of General Practice*. Now combine these sets by typing:

**3        1 and 2**

This gives you anything with "confidentiality" in the title *and* that was published in the *British Journal of General Practice*: a single article in three steps.[2] Note you can also combine sets in OVID by using the combine (Alt-C) key option.

You could have done all this in one step with the following command (try it now):

**4        confidentiality.ti and british journal of general practice.jn**

This step illustrates the use of the Boolean operator **"and"**, which will give you articles common to both sets. Use of the operator **"or"** will simply add the two sets together.

Note that you should not generally use abbreviations for journal titles in OVID, but other software packages may use standard abbreviations. Two important exceptions to this rule in OVID are the *Journal of the American Medical Association (JAMA)*, and the *British Medical Journal*, which changed its official title in 1988 to *BMJ*. To search for *BMJ* articles from 1988 to date, you must use

*BMJ;* for articles up to and including 1987 you should search under both *British Medical Journal* and *British Medical Journal clinical research ed.*

Often, you don't know the title of a paper but you know who wrote it. Alternatively, you may have been impressed with an article you have read (or lecture you heard) by a particular author and you want to see what else they have published. Clear your previous searches by selecting "edit" from the menu bar at the top of the main search screen, then choosing "delete all".

Let's try finding Professor Andy Haines' publications over the past five years. The syntax is as follows. Type:

1        **haines-a.au**

This gives you all articles on this part of the database in which A Haines is an author or coauthor—about 35 papers. But like many authors, Andy is not the only A Haines in the medical literature, and, another problem, he has a middle initial that he uses inconsistently in his publications. Unless you already know his middle initial, you must use a *truncation symbol* to find it out. Type:

2        **haines-a$.au**

This gives you about 50 articles, which include the previous 35 you found under A Haines, plus articles by AH Haines, AM Haines, and another 8 articles by—we've found him—AP Haines! Note that in OVID, the dollar sign is a truncation symbol meaning "any character or characters". With Silver Platter search software the equivalent symbol is an asterisk (*). You can use the truncation symbol to search a stem in a textword search, for example, the syntax **electric$.tw** (in OVID) will uncover articles with "electric", "electricity", "electrical", and so on in the title or abstract.

You could have used the following single line command:

3        **(haines-a or haines-ap).au**

This gives a total of around 40 articles, which you now need to browse by hand to exclude any A Haineses other than Prof Andy.

You may also find it helpful to search by institution field. This will give you all the papers that were produced in a particular research institution. For example, type:

4        **(withington hospital and manchester).in**

to find all the papers where "Withington Hospital, Manchester" appears in the "institution" field (either as the main address where the research was done or as that of one of the coauthors).

If you can't remember the title of the article you want but you know some exact key phrases from the abstract, it might be quicker to search under text words than MeSH terms (which are explained in the next section). The field suffixes you need are **.ti** (title), **.ab** (abstract), and **.tw** (textword = either title or abstract). Let's say you were trying to find an editorial from one of the medical journals (you can't remember which) in 1995 about evidence based medicine. Clear your previous searches, then type:

1        **evidence-based medicine.tw and 95.yr**

This gives you a total of about 60 articles. You could now browse the abstracts by hand to identify the one you are looking for. Alternatively, you could refine your search by publication type as follows. Type:

2        **limit 1 to editorial**

You could, in fact, have done all this in a single step with the following command:

3        **evidence-based medicine.tw and 95.yr and editorial.pt**

where **.tw** means "textword" (in title or abstract), **.yr** means "year of publication", and **.pt** means "publication type". (You could also have used the "limit set" option (Alt-M) here and then selected the publication type as "editorial".) Note, however, that this method will *only* pick up articles with the exact string "evidence based medicine" as a textword. It will miss, for example, articles that talk about "evidence based health care" instead of evidence based medicine. For this we need to search under MeSH terms, as explained below or cover all possible variations in the textwords (including different ways of spelling each word), or both.

---

## Exercise 1

1 Try to track down the following articles using as few commands as possible:

a) A paper by Husby and colleagues on the treatment of croup with nebulised budesonide (this was a double blind, placebo controlled study) published in one of the paediatric journals in about 1993. (Don't forget that the OVID system needs an initial for the author's name).

b) A paper by Professor Barker's team from Southampton on disproportionate fetal growth and raised IgE concentrations in adult life, published in a specialist allergy journal a couple of years ago. (Note that you do not need the full address of the institution to search under this field).

c) A study published in about 1993 in the *Lancet* on vertical transmission of HIV infection from mother to fetus, by a team from the Institute of Child Health.

d) Two articles published in 1995 in the *American Journal of Medical Genetics* on the inheritance of schizophrenia in Israeli subjects. See if you can find them in a single command using field suffixes.

2 Trace the series of articles published in the *Journal of the American Medical Association* between 1992 and 1997 entitled "Users' guides to the medical literature". Once you've found them, copy them and keep them. Much of the rest of this book is based on these users' guides.

3 How many articles can you find by Professor David Sackett, who, like Professor Haines, uses his middle initial inconsistently?

4 Find out how many articles have been published by Tony Delamothe in the *British Medical Journal* this year. Remember that to restrict your search to a particular year, use the "limit set" option (Alt-M) and then select "publication year", or, alternatively, use the field suffix **.yr** (for example, **94.yr**).

## 2.4 Problem 2—You want to answer a very specific clinical question

*Solution—Construct a focused (specific) search by combining two or more broad (sensitive) searches*

I was recently asked by the mother of a young girl with anorexia nervosa whose periods had ceased to put her on the pill so as to stop her bones thinning. This seemed a reasonable request, though there were ethical problems to consider. But is there any evidence that going on the pill in these circumstances really prevents long term bone loss? I decided to explore the subject using Medline. To answer this question, you need to search very broadly under "anorexia nervosa", "osteoporosis", and "oral contraceptives". First, clear your screen by erasing the previous searches. The search described below involves articles from 1992 so make sure the database you are searching goes back that far. Type:

1        **anorexia nervosa**

You have not typed a field suffix (such as **.tw**), so the OVID system will automatically try to "map" your request to one of its standard medical subject headings (abbreviated "MeSH" and colloquially known as "mesh terms"). (Note that not all Medicine software packages will automatically map your suggestion to MeSH terms. With Silver Platter search software, for example, you need to enter your heading and click the "suggest" button.) In this case, the screen offers you either "eating disorders" or "anorexia nervosa" and asks you to pick the closest one. Choose "anorexia nervosa" (space bar to highlight the text, then press "return").

The screen then asks you whether you want to "restrict to focus". Do you only want articles that are actually *about* anorexia nervosa or do you want any article that mentions anorexia nervosa in passing? Let's say we do want to restrict to focus. Next, the screen offers us a choice of subheadings, but we'll ignore these for a moment. Select "Include all subheadings". We could have got this far with a single line command as follows. Type:

2        ***anorexia nervosa/**

where * shows that the term is a major focus of the article and / represents a MeSH term. You should have about 750 articles in this set.

Similarly, to get articles on osteoporosis (which is also a MeSH term), use the following single line command:

3          osteoporosis/

You should get about 2200 articles. Note that in OVID, if you know that the subject you want is an official MeSH term you can cut the mapping process by typing a slash (/) after the word. This can save considerable time. Note also that we have not used an asterisk here, because osteoporosis may not be the focus of the article we are looking for.

Finally, put in the term "oral contraceptives" (without an asterisk and without a slash) to see what the MeSH term here is. You will be offered "contraceptives, oral", and if you had known this you could have used the following command:

4          contraceptives, oral/

This set should contain around 1200 articles. If you combine these three sets, either by using their set numbers 2 and 3 and 4 or by typing the single line command:

5          *anorexia nervosa/ and osteoporosis/ and
            contraceptives, oral/

you will have searched over 4000 articles and struck a single bull's eye[3]. (If you don't find it, check the syntax of your search carefully, then try running the same search through the previous five year database with the Alt-B command.)

## Exercise 2

Try to find a set of fewer than five articles relating to any of the following questions or clinical problems:

1  Is the high incidence of coronary heart disease in certain ethnic Asian groups attributable to differences in Lp(a) lipoprotein?

2  The hypothesis linking vitamin C with cure of the common cold is, apparently, something to do with its role as an antioxidant. Is there any (clinical or theoretical) evidence to support this hypothesis?

3  How should thyrotoxicosis be managed in pregnancy?

Make sure you practice finding the MeSH term for each subject, using the asterisk to restrict to focus, and using the slash to denote what you know is a MeSH term. (If the current database disappoints you, rerun your search on previous databases by selecting the database option, Alt-B.)

## 2.5 Problem 3—You want to get general information quickly about a well defined topic

*Solution—Use subheadings and/or the "limit set" options*

This is one of the commonest reasons why we approach Medline in real life. We don't have a particular paper in mind or a very specific question to ask and we aren't aiming for an exhaustive overview of the literature. We just want to know, say, what's the latest expert advice on drug treatment for asthma or whether anything new has been written on whooping cough vaccine.

One method to accomplish this is to search with MeSH terms and then, if we unearth a large number of articles *but not otherwise,* to use index subheadings. Subheadings are the fine tuning of the Medline indexing system and classify articles on a particular MeSH topic into aetiology, prevention, therapy, and so on. The most useful ones are listed in Box 2.2. I try not to use subheadings myself as my librarian colleagues tell me that an estimated 50% of articles in Medline are inadequately or incorrectly classified by subheading.

### Box 2.2 Useful subheadings (OVID)

| Syntax | Meaning | Example |
|--------|---------|---------|
| /ae | Adverse effects | **thalidomide/ae** |
| /co | Complications | **measles/co** |
| /ct | Contraindications (of drug) | **propranolol/ct** |
| /di | Diagnosis | **glioma/di** |
| /dt | Drug therapy of | **depression/dt** |
| /ed | Education | **asthma/ed** |
| /ep | Epidemiology | **poliomyelitis/ep** |
| /hi | History | **mastectomy/hi** |
| /nu | Nursing | **cerebral palsy/nu** |
| /og | Organisation/administration | **health service/og** |
| /pc | Prevention and control | **influenza/pc** |
| /px | Psychology | **diabetes/px** |
| /th | Therapy | **hypertension/th** |
| /tu | Therapeutic use (of drug) | **aspirin/tu** |

Note that the subheading **/th** in Box 2.2 refers to the non-pharmacological therapy of a disease, whereas **/dt** is used for drug therapy. The subheading **/tu** is used exclusively for drugs and means "therapeutic use of". The subheading **/px** is used with non-psychiatric diseases as in this example—**diabetes/px** = psychology of diabetes.

Not all subheadings are used in the indexing system for every topic. To find the subheadings for a MeSH term such as asthma, with a view to finding new drug treatments, type:

1        **sh asthma**

This command will tell you which subheadings are used in the indexing system for this MeSH term. It gives you a number of options, including diagnosis, economics, ethnology, and so on. You should choose **/dt** (drug therapy). You could have typed the single line command:

2        **\*asthma/dt**

where **\*** denotes a major focus of the article, **/** denotes a MeSH term, and **dt** means drug therapy. This will give you around 1800 articles to choose from. You now need to *limit the set*, so select the "limit set" option (Alt-M). You must choose, one at a time, options for cutting the set down to a number that you can browse comfortably. It actually doesn't take long to browse through 50 or so articles on the screen. It is better to do this than to rely on the software to give you the best of the bunch. In other words, don't overapply the "limit set" commands you find in Box 2.3.

If you are sure you want a review article, select this option. You can get the latest review by selecting first "review articles" and then "latest update". However, given that the very latest update may not be the best overview written in the past year or so, you may be better selecting "publication year" as the current year and trawling through. Remember that only a *systematic review* will have involved and will include details of a thorough search of the relevant literature (see chapter 8).

If you actually want to copy a full article today, select "local holdings". This will restrict your set to journals that are held in the particular library through which you are accessing Medline. If you access Medline at the BMA library via a computer modem, "local holdings" means journals held at the BMA library not the library where you are dialling from. Note that options such as "local holdings" reduce your article count in a non-systematic way—there are probably many excellent and relevant articles published in journals that your local library does not take.

---

**Box 2.3 Useful "limit set" options**

| | | |
|---|---|---|
| AIM journals | Review articles | English language |
| Nursing journals | Editorials | Male/Female |
| Dental journals | Abstracts | Human |
| Cancer journals | Local holdings | Publication year |

---

The option "AIM journals" denotes all journals listed in the *Abridged Index Medicus*—that is, the "mainstream" medical journals. Alternatively, if you want articles relating to nursing rather than medical care you could limit the set to "Nursing journals". This is often a better way of limiting a large set than asking for local holdings. If you are not interested in seeing anything in a foreign language (even though the abstract may be in English), select this option, again bearing in mind that it is a non-systematic (indeed, a very biased) way of excluding articles from your set[4].

Note that instead of using the "limit set" function key you can use direct single line commands such as:

3  **limit 4 to local holdings**

4  **limit 5 to human**

---

**Exercise 3**

Try to find a single paper (by browsing a larger set) to give you a quick answer to the following questions:

1 Does hormone replacement therapy cause an increased incidence of breast cancer?

2 The north American medical literature often mentions Health Maintenance Organizations. What are these?

3 Imagine that you are a medical journalist who has been asked to write an article on prostate cancer. You want two fairly short review articles, from the mainstream medical literature, to use as your sources.

4 Does watching violence on television lead to violent behaviour in adolescents?

---

## 2.6 Problem 4—Your search gives you lots of irrelevant articles

*Solution—Refine your search as you go along in the light of interim results*

Often, a search uncovers dozens of articles that are irrelevant to your question. The Boolean operator **"not"** can help here. I recently undertook a search to identify articles on surrogate end points in clinical pharmacology research. I searched Medline by MeSH terms but I also wanted to search by textwords to pick up articles that the MeSH indexing system had missed (see section 2.7). Unfortunately, my search revealed hundreds of articles I didn't want—all on surrogate motherhood. (Surrogate end points are explained in section 6.3, but the point here is they are nothing to do with surrogate motherhood.) The syntax to exclude the unwanted articles is as follows:

1      **(surrogate not mother$).tw**

Deciding to use the **"not"** operator is a good example of how you can (and should) refine your search as you go along—much easier than producing the perfect search off the top of your head. Another way of getting rid of irrelevant articles is to narrow your textword search to adjacent words. For example, the term "home help" includes two very common words linked in a specific context. Link them as follows.

2      **home adj help.tw**

where adj means "adjacent". Similarly, "community adj care", "Macmillan adj nurse". You can even specify the number of words gap between two linked words, as in:

3      **community adj2 care.tw**

which would find "community mental health care" as well as "community child care" and "community care".

25

**Exercise 4**

1   Find articles about occupational asthma caused by sugar.

2   The drug chloroquine is most commonly used for the treatment of falciparum malaria. Find out what other uses it has. (Hint: use the subheading **/tu,** which means "therapeutic use of" and remember that malaria is often referred to by its Latin name *plasmodium falciparum.* You should, of course, limit a large search to review articles if you are reading for quick information rather than secondary research.)

## 2.7   Problem 5—Your search gives you no articles at all or not as many as you expected

*Solution—First, don't overuse subheadings or the "limit set" options; second, search under textwords as well as MeSH terms; third, learn about the "explode" command, and use it routinely*

If your carefully constructed search bears little or no fruit, it is possible that there are no relevant articles in the database. More likely, you have missed them. Many important articles are missed not because we constructed a flawed search strategy but because we relied too heavily on a flawed indexing system. I've already talked about the overuse of subheadings (see section 2.5). MeSH terms may also be wrongly assigned or not assigned at all. For this reason, you should adopt a "belt and braces" approach and search under textwords as well as by MeSH. After all, it's difficult to write an article on the psychology of diabetes without mentioning the words "diabetes", "diabetic", "psychology", or "psychological", so the truncation stems **diabet$.tw** and **psychol$.tw** would supplement a search under the MeSH term "diabetes mellitus" and the subheading **/px** (psychology).

Clear your screen, then consider this example. If you wanted to answer the question: What is the role of aspirin in the prevention and treatment of myocardial infarction? you could type the single line command:

1        **(myocardial infarction/pc or myocardial infarction/dt) and aspirin/tu**

which would give you all articles listed in this part of the Medline

26

database that cover the therapeutic use of aspirin and the prevention or treatment of myocardial infarction—190 or so articles—but no immediate answer to your question. You might be better dropping the subheadings and limiting the set as follows:

1    **myocardial infarction/ and aspirin/**

2    **limit 1 to human**

3    **limit 2 to AIM journals**

4    **limit 3 to review articles**

a strategy that would give you around 25 review articles, including at least three very useful ones that your first search (by subheadings) missed. Now, let's add an extra string to this strategy. Erase the set so far, and work as follows:

1    **myocardial infarction/ and aspirin/**

2    **(myocardial infarct$ or heart attack).tw and aspirin.tw**

3    **1 or 2**

4    **limit 3 to human**

5    **limit 4 to AIM journals**

6    **limit 5 to review articles**

This last, more refined, search, which included key textwords, gives you over 50 articles, most of which look very relevant to your question and many of which were missed when you searched MeSH terms alone.

Another important strategy for preventing incomplete searches is to use the powerful "explode" command. The MeSH terms are like the branches of a tree, with, for example, "inflammatory bowel disease" subdividing into "ulcerative colitis", "Crohn's disease", and so on. Medline indexers are instructed to index items by using the most specific MeSH terms they can. If you just ask for articles on "inflammatory bowel disease" you will miss all the terminal divisions of the branch unless you "explode" the term. (Note, however, that you can explode a term only *down* the MeSH tree, not upwards.) Try the following search as an example. We are trying to get hold of a good review article about breast cancer in men. Clear your screen, then type the MeSH term:

**1    breast neoplasms/**

This will give you about 15 000 articles. You could narrow the search down using the "limit set" option (Alt-M) "male", "human", and so on, or by typing:

**2    limit 1 to male**

**3    limit 2 to human**

**4    limit 3 to AIM journals**

**5    limit 4 to review articles**

This narrows your search drastically to around 37 articles, none of which offers a comprehensive overview of the subject. And how many have you missed? The answer is quite a few of them, because the MeSH term "breast neoplasms" subdivides into several branches, including "breast neoplasms, male". Try it all again (without erasing the first search), but this time, explode the term "breast neoplasms" before you start:

**6    exp breast neoplasms/**

**7    limit 6 to male**

**8    limit 7 to human**

**9    limit 8 to AIM journals**

**10    limit 9 to review articles**

You now have around 35 articles, including a major overview[5], which your unexploded search missed. You can demonstrate this by typing:

**11    10 not 5**

which will show you what the exploded search revealed over and above the unexploded one. Incidentally, if you were also thinking of searching under textwords, the syntax for identifying articles about the problem in men would be **(male not female).tw** and **(men not women).tw** as the female terms here literally incorporate the male.

## 2.8 Problem 6—You don't know where to start searching

*Solution—Use the "permuted index" option*

Let's take the term "stress". It comes up a lot but searching for particular types of stress would be laborious and searching "stress" as a textword would be too unfocused. We need to know where in the MeSH index the various types of stress lie, and when we see that we can choose the sort of stress we want to look at. For this, we use the command **ptx** ("permuted index"). Type:

1      **ptx stress**

The screen shows many options, including post-traumatic stress disorders, stress fracture, oxidative stress, stress incontinence, and so on. **ptx** is a useful command when the term you are exploring might be found in several subject areas. If your subject word *is* a discrete MeSH term, use the **tree** command. For example:

2      **tree epilepsy**

will show where epilepsy is placed in the MeSH index (as a branch of "brain diseases"), which itself branches into generalised epilepsy, partial epilepsy, post-traumatic epilepsy, and so on.

### Exercise 5

1  Find where the word "nursing" might appear as part of a MeSH term.

2  Use the "tree" command to expand the MeSH term "diabetes mellitus".

## 2.9 Problem 7—Your attempt to limit a set leads to loss of important articles but does not exclude those of low methodological quality

*Solution—Apply an EBQF (evidence based quality filter)*

What do you do when your closely focused search still gives you several hundred articles to choose from and if applying subheadings or limit set functions seems to lose valuable (and valid) papers? Firstly, you should consider the possibility that your search wasn't as focused as you thought. But if you can't improve on it you should try inserting a quality string designed to limit your set to therapeutic interventions, aetiology, diagnostic procedures, or epidemiology. Alternatively, you could apply search strings to identify the publication type, such as randomised controlled trial, systematic review, or meta-analysis.

These EBQFs (evidence based quality filters), which are listed in appendices B and C, are highly complex search strategies developed and refined by some of the world's most experienced medical information experts. I am grateful to the UK Cochrane Centre for permission to reproduce them here. You can copy them into your personal computer and save them as cut-and-paste strategies to be added to your subject searches.

---

**Exercise 6**

1 Search for a good randomised controlled trial of the use of aspirin in the treatment of acute myocardial infarction.

2 Find a systematic review on the risk of gastrointestinal bleeding with non-steroidal anti-inflammatory drugs.

---

## 2.10 Problem 8—Medline hasn't helped, despite a thorough search

*Solution—Explore other medical and paramedical databases*

Entry of articles on to the Medline database is open to human error, both from authors and editors who select key words for indexing, and from librarians who group articles under subheadings and type in the abstracts. According to one estimate, 40% of material that should be listed on Medline can, in reality, be accessed only by looking through all the journals again, by hand. Furthermore, a number of important medical and paramedical journals are not covered by Medline at all. It is said that Medline lacks comprehensive references in the fields of psychology, medical sociology, and non-clinical pharmacology.

If you want to broaden your search to other electronic databases, ask your local librarian where you could access the following:

● *AIDSLINE* references the literature on AIDS and HIV back to 1980

- *Allied and Alternative Medicine* covers a range of complementary and alternative medicine including homeopathy, chiropractic, acupuncture, and so on
- *American Medical Association Journals* provides the full text of JAMA plus 10 specialty journals produced by the American Medical Association from 1982
- *ASSIA* is an applied social sciences database covering psychology, sociology, politics, and economics since 1987; all documents have abstracts
- *Cancer-CD* is a compilation by Silver Platter of CANCERLIT and Embase cancer related records from 1984. The CD ROM version is updated quarterly
- *CINAHL* is the nursing and allied health database covering all aspects of nursing, health education, occupational therapy, social services in health care, and other related disciplines from 1983. The CD ROM version is updated monthly
- *Cochrane library*—the Cochrane Controlled Trials Register (CCTR), Cochrane Database of Systematic Reviews (CDSR), Database of Abstracts of Reviews of Effectiveness (DARE), and Cochrane Review Methodology Database (CRMD) are updated quarterly; authors of systematic reviews on CDSR undertake to update their own contributions periodically. See text for further details
- *Current Contents Search* indexes journal issues on or before their publication date. It is useful when checking for the very latest output on a subject. Updated weekly. From 1990
- *Current Research in Britain* is a UK wide database of academic research in progress
- *DHData* (formerly DHSS-Data), the database of the UK Department of Health, indexes articles covering health service and hospital administration from 1983
- *EmBase,* the database of Excerpta Medica, focuses on drugs and pharmacology but also includes other biomedical specialties. It is more up to date than Medline and with better European coverage. The CD ROM version is updated monthly
- *HELMIS,* the Health Management Information Service at the Nuffield Institute of Health, Leeds, indexes articles on health service management
- *National Research Register (UK)* is a new database of information about research and development projects taking place in, or of

interest to, the UK NHS. There are plans to incorporate the NHS research and development database and the Medical Research Council projects database and clinical trials directory.

● *Psyclit* is produced by the America Psychological Association as the computer searchable version of Psychological Abstracts. It covers psychology, psychiatry, and related subjects; journals are included from 1974 and books from 1987 (English language only)

● *Science citation index* indexes the references cited in articles as well as the usual author, title, abstract, and citation of the articles themselves. Useful for finding follow up work done on a key article and for tracking down the addresses of authors

● *SHARE,* a database, funded by the UK Department of Health and based at the King's Fund library in London, of published and ongoing research into the health of and health services for black and minority ethnic groups

● *Toxline* has information on toxicological effects of chemicals and drugs on living systems, from 1981

● *UNICORN* is the main database of the King's Fund, London. Covers a range of journals on health, health management, health economics, and social sciences. Particularly strong on primary health care and the health of Londoners.

Of all these, the one to watch is, I believe, the Cochrane library. In 1972, epidemiologist Archie Cochrane called for the establishment of a central international register of clinical trials. (It was Cochrane who, as a rebellious young medical student, marched through the streets of London in 1938 bearing a placard that stated, "All effective treatments should be free". His book *Effectiveness and efficiency* caused little reaction at the time but captures the essence of today's evidence based medicine movement[6].)

Though he never lived to see the eponym, Archie Cochrane's vision of a reliable, comprehensive and accurate medical database, the Cochrane Controlled Trials Register, is approaching reality. The Cochrane library also includes two "metadatabases" (the Cochrane Database of Systematic Reviews and the Database of Abstracts of Reviews of Effectiveness) and a fourth database on the science of research synthesis (the Cochrane Review Methodology Database). This entire library is available on CD ROM from the BMA bookshop.

Published articles are entered on to the Cochrane databases by members of the Cochrane Collaboration[6], an international network of (mostly) medically qualified volunteers who each take on the handsearching of a particular clinical journal back to the very first issue. Using strict methodological criteria, the handsearchers classify each article according to publication type (randomised trial, other controlled clinical trial, epidemiological survey, and so on) and prepare structured abstracts in house style. The collaboration has already identified over 30 000 trials that had not been appropriately tagged in Medline[6].

At the time of writing, the Cochrane library is far from comprehensive, but by 2000 it will probably have replaced Medline as the medical researcher's first port of call. The databases are in user friendly Windows-style format; numerical data in overviews are presented in standardised graphics way to allow busy clinicians to assess their relevance quickly and objectively. Watch this space!

[1] Jones R, Kinmonth A-L. *Critical reading for primary care.* Oxford; Oxford University Press, 1995.

[2] Carmen D, Britten N. Confidentiality and medical records: the patient's perspective. *Brit J Gen Pract* 1995, **45**: 485–8.

[3] Seeman E, Szmukler GI, Formica C, *et al.* Osteoporosis in anorexia nervosa: the influence of peak bone density, bone loss, oral contraceptive use, and exercise. *J Bone Min Res* 1992; **7**: 1467-74.

[4] Moher D, Fortin P, Jadad AR, *et al.* Completeness of reporting of trials published in languages other than English: implications for conduct and reporting of systematic reviews. *Lancet* 1996; **347**: 363-6.

[5] Hecht JR, Winchester DJ. Male breast cancer. *Am J Clin Path* 1994; **102**: 525-30.

[6] Cochrane A. *Effectiveness and efficiency.* London: Nuffield Provincial Hospitals Trust, 1972.

[7] Pore T, Dunio D. The Cochrane Collaboration: preparing, maintaining, and disseminating systematic reviews of the effects of health care. *JAMA* 1995; **274**: 1935-8.

# Chapter 3: Getting your bearings (what is this paper about?)

## 3.1 The science of "trashing" papers

It usually comes as a surprise to students to learn that some (the purists would say up to 99% of) published articles belong in the bin and should certainly not be used to inform practice. In 1979, the editor of the BMJ, Dr Stephen Lock, wrote "Few things are more dispiriting to a medical editor than having to reject a paper based on a good idea but with irremediable flaws in the methods used". Things have improved since then, but not enormously[1] (see Box 3.1).

Most papers appearing in medical journals these days are presented more or less in standard IMRAD format: Introduction (*why* the authors decided to do this particular piece of research), Methods (*how* they did it and how they chose to analyse their results), Results (*what* they found), and Discussion (what they think the results *mean*). If you are deciding whether a paper is worth reading, you should do so on the design of the methods section and not on the interest value of the hypothesis, the nature or potential impact of the results, or the speculation in the discussion.

Conversely, bad science is bad science regardless of whether the study examined an important clinical issue, whether the results are "statistically significant" (see section 5.5), whether things changed in the direction you would have liked them to, and whether, if true, the findings promise immeasurable benefits for patients or savings for the health service. Strictly speaking, *if you are going to trash a paper, you should do so before you even look at the results.*

34

---

**Box 3.1 Common reasons why papers are rejected for publication**

- The study did not examine an important scientific issue (see section 3.2)

- The study was not original—that is, someone else has already done the same or a similar study (see section 4.1)

- The study did not actually test the authors' hypothesis (see section 3.2)

- A different type of study should have been done (see section 3.3)

- Practical difficulties (for example, in recruiting subjects) led the authors to compromise on the original study protocol (see section 4.3)

- The sample size was too small (see section 4.6)

- The study was uncontrolled or inadequately controlled (see section 4.4)

- The statistical analysis was incorrect or inappropriate (see chapter 5)

- The authors have drawn unjustified conclusions from their data

- There is a considerable conflict of interest (for example, one of the authors or a sponsor might benefit financially from the publication of the paper and insufficient safeguards were seen to be in place to guard against bias)

- The paper is so badly written that it is incomprehensible

---

It is much easier to pick holes in other people's work than to do a methodologically perfect piece of research oneself. When I teach critical appraisal there is usually someone in the group who finds it profoundly discourteous to criticise research projects into which dedicated scientists have put the best years of their lives. On a more pragmatic note, there may be good practical reasons why the authors of the study have "cut corners" and they know as well as you do that their work would have been more scientifically valid if they hadn't.

Most good scientific journals send papers out to a referee for comments on their scientific validity, originality, and importance before deciding whether to print them. This process is know as *peer review*, and much has been written about it[2]. Common defects picked up by referees are listed in box 3.1.

I recently corresponded with an author whose paper I had refereed (anonymously, though I subsequently declared myself) and recommended that it should not be published. On reading my report, he wrote to the editor and admitted he agreed with my opinion. He described five years of painstaking and unpaid research done mostly in his spare time and the gradual realisation that he had been testing an important hypothesis with the wrong method. He informed the editor that he was "withdrawing the paper with a wry smile and a heavy heart" and pointed out several further weaknesses of his study that I and the other referee had missed. He bears us no grudge and, like Kipling's hero, has now stooped to start anew with worn out tools. His paper remains unpublished, but he is a true (and rare) scientist.

The assessment of methodological quality (critical appraisal) has been covered in detail in many textbooks on evidence based medicine[3-7] and in Sackett and colleagues' *"Users' guides to the medical literature"* in the Journal of the American Medical Association[8-21]. The structured guides produced by these authors on how to read papers on therapy, diagnosis, screening, prognosis, causation, quality of care, economic analysis, and overview are regarded by many as the definitive checklists for critical appraisal. Appendix A lists some simpler checklists that I have derived from the users' guides and the other sources cited at the end of this chapter, together with some ideas of my own. If you are an experienced journal reader, these checklists will be largely self explanatory. If, however, you still have difficulty getting started when looking at a medical paper, try asking the preliminary questions in the next section.

## 3.2 Three preliminary questions to get your bearings

*Question 1—Why was the study done and what hypotheses were the authors testing?*

The introductory sentence of a research paper should state, in a nutshell, what the background to the research is. For example, "Grommet insertion is a common procedure in children, and it has been suggested that not all operations are clinically necessary". This statement should be followed by a brief review of the published literature, for example, "Gupta and Brown's prospective survey of grommet insertions demonstrated that...". It is irritatingly common for authors to forget to place their research in context as the background to the problem is usually clear as daylight to them by the time they reach the writing up stage.

Unless it has already been covered in the introduction, the methods section of the paper should state clearly the hypothesis that the authors have decided to test, such as "This study aimed to determine whether day case hernia surgery was safer and more acceptable to patients than the standard inpatient procedure". Again, this important step may be omitted or, more commonly, buried somewhere mid-paragraph. If the hypothesis is presented in the negative (which it usually is), such as "the addition of metformin to maximal dose sulphonylurea therapy will not improve the control of type 2 diabetes", it is known as a *null* hypothesis.

The authors of a study rarely actually *believe* their null hypothesis when they embark on their research. Being human, they have usually set out to demonstrate a difference between the two arms of their study. But the way scientists do this is to say "let's *assume* there's no difference; now let's try to disprove that theory". If you adhere to the teachings of Karl Popper, this *hypotheticodeductive* approach (setting up falsifiable hypotheses that you then proceed to test) is the very essence of the scientific method[22].

If you have not discovered what the authors' stated (or unstated) hypothesis was by the time you are halfway through the methods section you may find it in the first paragraph of the discussion. Remember, however, that not all research studies (even good ones) ιιιι ιι ι ιιμι ισ ιεει ιι ειιιμισ αειιιιιινε hypothesis. *Qualitative* research studies, which are as valid and as necessary as the more conventional quantitative studies, aim to look at particular issues in a broad, open ended way to generate (or modify) hypotheses and prioritise areas to investigate. This type of research is discussed further in chapter 11. Even quantitative research (which the rest of this book is about) is now seen as more than hypothesis testing. As section 5.5 argues, it is strictly preferable to talk about evaluating the *strength* of evidence around a particular issue than about proving or disproving hypotheses.

*Question 2—What type of study was done?*

First, decide whether the paper describes a primary or secondary study. Primary studies report research first hand, while secondary (or *integrative*) studies attempt to summarise and draw conclusions from primary studies. Primary studies, the stuff of most published research in medical and nursing journals, usually fall into one of three categories:

- *Experiments*, in which a manoeuvre is performed on an animal or a volunteer in artificial and controlled surroundings

- *Clinical trials*, in which an intervention, such as a drug treatment, is offered to a group of patients who are then followed up to see what happens to them

- *Surveys*, in which something is measured in a group of patients, health professionals, or some other sample of individuals.

The commoner types of clinical trials and surveys are discussed in the later sections of this chapter. Make sure you understand any jargon used in describing the study design (see box 3.2).

Secondary research comprises:

- *Overviews*, which are considered in chapter 8, may be divided into

  - *(Non-systematic) reviews*, which summarise primary studies

  - *Systematic reviews*, which do this according to a rigorous and predefined methodology

  - *Meta-analyses*, which integrate the numerical data from more than one study

- *Guidelines*, which are considered in chapter 9, draw conclusions from primary studies about how clinicians should be behaving

- *Decision analyses*, which are not discussed in detail in this book but are covered elsewhere[24-26], use the results of primary studies to generate probability trees to be used by both health professionals and patients in making choices about clinical management

- *Economic analyses*, which are considered in chapter 10, use the results of primary studies to say whether a particular course of action is a good use of resources.

## Box 3.2 Terms used to describe design features of clinical research studies

| Term | Meaning |
| --- | --- |
| Parallel group comparison | Each group receives a different treatment, with both groups being entered at the same time. In this case, results are analysed by comparing groups |
| Paired (or matched) comparison | Subjects receiving different treatments are matched to balance potential confounding variables such as age and sex. Results are analysed in terms of differences between subject pairs |
| Within subject comparison | Subjects are assessed before and after an intervention and results analysed in terms of within subject changes |
| Single blind | Subjects did not know which treatment they were receiving |
| Double blind | Neither investigators nor subjects knew who was receiving which treatment |
| Crossover | Each subject received both the intervention and control treatments (in random order) often separated by a *washout* period on no treatment |
| Placebo controlled | Control subjects receive a placebo (inactive pill), which should look and taste the same as the active pill. Placebo (sham) operations may also be used in trials of surgery |
| Factorial design | A study that permits investigation of the effects (both separately and combined) of more than one independent variable on a given outcome (for example, a 2 x 2 factorial design tested the effects of placebo, aspirin alone, streptokinase alone, or aspirin plus streptokinase in acute heart attack[23]) |

*Question 3—Was this design appropriate to the broad field of research studied?*

Examples of the sorts of questions that can reasonably be answered by different types of primary research study are given in the sections that follow. One question that frequently cries out to be asked is this: Was a randomised controlled trial (see section 3.3 below) the best method of testing this particular hypothesis, and if the study was not a randomised controlled trial, should it have been? Before you jump to any conclusions, decide what broad field of research the study covers (see box 3.3). Once you have done this, ask whether the right type of study was done to examine a question in this field.

---

### Box 3.3 Broad topics of research

Most research studies are concerned with one or more of the following:

- *Therapy*—testing the efficacy of drug treatments, surgical procedures, alternative methods of patient education, or other interventions. Preferred study design is randomised controlled trial (see section 3.3 and chapter 6)

- *Diagnosis*—demonstrating whether a new diagnostic test is valid (can we trust it?) and reliable (would we get the same results every time?). Preferred study design is cross sectional survey (see section 3.6 and chapter 7) in which both the new test and the gold standard test are performed

- *Screening*—demonstrating the value of tests that can be applied to large populations and that pick up disease at a presymptomatic stage. Preferred study design is cross sectional survey (see section 3.6 and chapter 7)

- *Prognosis*—determining what is likely to happen to someone whose disease is picked up at an early stage. Preferred study design is longitudinal cohort study (see section 3.7)

- *Causation*—determining whether a putative harmful agent, such as environmental pollution, is related to the development of illness. Preferred study design is cohort or case-control study, depending on how rare the disease is (see sections 3.4 and 3.5), but case reports (see section 3.7) may also provide crucial information

---

## 3.3 Randomised controlled trials

In a randomised controlled trial participants in the trial are randomly allocated, by a process equivalent to the flip of a coin, to either one intervention (such as a drug treatment) or another (such as placebo treatment). Both groups are followed up for a specified time period and analysed in terms of specific outcomes defined at the outset of the study (for example, death, heart attack, serum cholesterol concentration, etc). Because, *on average*, the groups are identical apart from the intervention any differences in outcome are, in theory, attributable to the intervention. In reality, however, not every randomised controlled trial is a bowl of cherries.

Some papers that report trials that compare an intervention with a control group are not, in fact, randomised trials at all. The terminology for these is *other controlled clinical trials*, a term used to

---

**Box 3.4 Advantages of the randomised controlled trial design**

- Allows rigorous evaluation of a single variable (for example, effect of drug treatment versus placebo) in a precisely defined patient group (for example, menopausal women aged 50-60 years)

- Prospective design (that is, data are collected on events that happen *after* you decide to do the study)

- Uses hypotheticodeductive reasoning (that is, seeks to falsify, rather than confirm, its own hypothesis; see section 3.2)

- Potentially eradicates bias by comparing two otherwise identical groups (but see below and section 4.4)

- Allows for meta-analysis (combining the numerical results of several similar trials) at a later date; see section 8.3

---

describe comparative studies in which subjects were allocated to intervention or control groups in a non-random manner. This may arise, for example, when random allocation would be impossible, impractical, or unethical—for example, in a trial to compare the outcome of childbirth with or without the father present. The problems of non-random allocation are discussed further in section 4.4 in relation to determining whether the two groups in a trial can reasonably be compared with one another on a statistical level.

Some trials count as a sort of halfway house between true randomised trials and non-randomised trials. In these, randomisation is not done truly at random (for example, using sequentially numbered sealed envelopes each with a computer generated random number inside) but by some method that allows the clinician to know which group the patient would be in *before he or she makes a definitive decision to randomise the patient.* This allows subtle biases to creep in as the clinician might be more (or less) likely to enter a particular patient into the trial if he or she believed that the patient would get active treatment. In particular, patients with more severe disease may be subconsciously withheld from the placebo arm of the trial. Examples of unacceptable methods include randomisation by last digit of date of birth (even numbers to group A, etc), toss of a coin, sequential allocation (patient A to group 1; patient B to group 2, etc), and date seen in clinic (all patients seen this week to group A; all those seen next week to group 2, etc)[27].

Listed below are examples of clinical questions that would be best answered by a randomised controlled trial, but note also the examples in the later sections of this chapter of situations when other types of study could or must be used instead.

- Is this drug better than placebo or a different drug for a particular disease?
- Is a new surgical procedure better than currently favoured practice?
- Is a leaflet better than verbal advice in helping patients make informed choices about the treatment options for a particular condition?
- Will changing from a margarine high in saturated fats to one high in polyunsaturated fats significantly affect serum cholesterol concentrations?

Randomised controlled trials are said to be the gold standard in medical research. Up to a point this is true (see section 3.8) but only for certain types of clinical question (see box 3.3 and sections 3.4 to 3.7). The questions that best lend themselves to this design are all about *interventions* and are mainly concerned with treatment or prevention. It should be remembered, however, that even when we are looking at therapeutic interventions, and especially when we are not, there are several important disadvantages associated with randomised trials (see box 3.5)[28].

> ## Box 3.5 Disadvantages of the randomised controlled trial design
>
> Expensive and time consuming, hence, in practice:
>
> - Many trials are either never done, are performed on too few subjects, or are undertaken for too short a period (see section 4.6)
>
> - Most trials are funded by large research bodies (university or government-sponsored) or drug companies, who ultimately dictate the research agenda
>
> - Surrogate end points are often used in preference to clinical outcome measures (see section 6.3)
>
> May introduce "hidden bias", especially through:
>
> - Imperfect randomisation (see above)
>
> - Failure to randomise all eligible patients (clinician offers participation in the trial only to patients he or she considers will respond well to the intervention)
>
> - Failure to blind assessors to randomisation status of patients (see section 4.5)

Remember, too, that the results of a randomised controlled trial may have limited applicability as a result of exclusion criteria (rules about who may not be entered into the study), inclusion bias (selection of trial subjects from a group that is unrepresentative of everyone with the condition (see section 4.2)), refusal of certain patient groups to give consent to be included in the trial[29], analysis of only predefined "objective" end points that may exclude important qualitative aspects of the intervention (see chapter 11), and publication bias (that is, the selective publication of positive results)[30]. While these problems might also occur with other trial designs, they may be particularly pertinent when a randomised controlled trial is being sold to you as, methodologically speaking, whiter than white.

There are, in addition, many situations in which randomised controlled trials are either unnecessary, impractical, or inappropriate:

*Randomised controlled trials are unnecessary*

- When a clearly successful intervention for an otherwise fatal condition is discovered

- When a previous randomised controlled trial or meta-analysis has given a definitive result (either positive or negative, see section 5.5). Some people would argue that it is actually *unethical* to ask patients to be randomised to a clinical trial without first conducting a systematic literature review to see whether the trial needs to be done at all.

*Randomised controlled trials are impractical*

- When it would be unethical to seek consent to randomise[31].

- When the number of subjects needed to demonstrate a significant difference between the groups is prohibitively high (see section 4.6).

*Randomised controlled trials are inappropriate*

- When the study is looking at the prognosis of a disease. For this analysis, the appropriate route to best evidence is a longitudinal survey of a properly assembled *inception cohort* (see section 3.6)

- When the study is looking at the validity of a diagnostic or screening test. For this analysis, the appropriate route to best evidence is a *cross sectional survey* of patients clinically suspected of harbouring the relevant disorder (see section 3.6 and chapter 7)

- When the study is looking at a "quality of care" issue in which the criteria for "success" have not yet been established. For example, a randomised controlled trial comparing medical versus surgical methods of abortion might assess "success" in terms of number of patients achieving complete evacuation, amount of bleeding, and pain level. The patients, however, might decide that other aspects of the procedure are important, such as knowing in advance how long the procedure will take, not seeing or feeling the abortus come out, and so on. For this analysis, the appropriate route to best evidence is a *qualitative research method*[32][33] (see chapter 11).

All these issues have been discussed in great depth by the clinical epidemiologists[3][6], who remind us that to turn our noses up at the non-randomised trial may indicate scientific naivety and not, as many people routinely assume, intellectual rigour. Note also that there is now a recommended format for reporting randomised controlled trials in medical journals that you should try to follow if you are writing one up yourself[34].

# 3.4 Cohort studies

In a cohort study, two (or more) groups of people are selected on the basis of differences in their exposure to a particular agent (such as a vaccine, a medicine, or an environmental toxin) and followed up to see how many in each group develop a particular disease or other outcome. The follow up period in cohort studies is generally measured in years (and sometimes in decades) as that is how long many diseases, especially cancer, take to develop. Note that randomised controlled trials are usually begun on *patients* (people who already have a disease) whereas most cohort studies are begun on *subjects* who may or may not develop disease.

A special type of cohort study may also be used to determine the prognosis (that is, what is likely to happen to someone who has it) of a disease. A group of patients who have all been diagnosed as having an early stage of the disease or have a positive result on a screening test (see chapter 7) is assembled (the inception cohort) and followed up on repeated occasions to see the incidence (new cases per year) and time course of different outcomes. (Here is a definition that you should commit to memory if you can: *incidence* is the number of new cases of a disease per year, whereas *prevalence* is the overall proportion of the population who suffer from the disease.)

The world's most famous cohort study, which won its two original authors a knighthood, was undertaken by Sir Austen Bradford Hill, Sir Richard Doll and, latterly, Richard Peto. They followed up 40 000 British doctors divided into four cohorts (non-smokers and light, moderate, and heavy smokers) by using both all cause (any death) and cause specific (death from a particular disease) mortality as outcome measures. Publication of their 10 year interim results in 1964, which showed a substantial excess in both mortality from lung cancer and all cause mortality in smokers, with a "dose-response" relation (that is, the more you smoke, the greater are your chances of getting lung cancer)[35], went a long way to demonstrating that the link between smoking and ill health was causal rather than coincidental. The 20 year[36] and 40 year[37] results of this momentous study (which achieved an impressive 94% follow up of those recruited in 1951 and not known to have died) illustrate both the perils of smoking and the strength of evidence that can be obtained from a properly conducted cohort study.

Clinical questions that should be examined by a cohort study include:

- Does the contraceptive pill "cause" breast cancer? (Note, once again, that the word "cause" is a loaded and potentially misleading term. As John Guillebaud has argued in his excellent book *The Pill*[38] if a thousand women went on the pill tomorrow, some of them would get breast cancer. But some of those would have got it anyway. The question that epidemiologists try to answer through cohort studies is, "What is the additional risk of developing breast cancer that this woman would run by taking the pill, over and above her 'baseline' risk attributable to her own hormonal balance, family history, diet, alcohol intake, and so on?")

- Does smoking cause lung cancer?[37]

- Does high blood pressure get better over time?

- What happens to infants who have been born very prematurely, in terms of subsequent physical development and educational achievement?

## 3.5 Case-control studies

In a case-control study, patients with a particular disease or condition are identified and "matched" with controls (patients with some other disease, the general population, neighbours, or relatives). Data are then collected (for example, by searching back through these people's medical records or by asking them to recall their own history) on past exposure to a possible causal agent for the disease. Like cohort studies, case-control studies are generally concerned with the aetiology of a disease (that is, what causes it) rather than its treatment. They lie lower down the hierarchy of evidence (see section 3.8), but this design is usually the only option in the study of rare conditions. An important source of difficulty (and potential bias) in a case-control study is the precise definition of who counts as a "case" since one misallocated subject may substantially influence the results (see section 4.4). In addition, such a design cannot demonstrate causality—in other words, the *association* of A with B in a case-control study does not prove that A has *caused* B (see page 80).

Clinical questions that should be examined by a case-control study include:

- Does the prone sleeping position increase the risk of cot death (the sudden infant death syndrome)?

- Does whooping cough vaccine cause brain damage? (see section 4.4)

- Do overhead power cables cause leukaemia?

## 3.6 Cross sectional surveys

We have probably all been asked to take part in a survey, even if it was only someone in the street asking us which brand of toothpaste we prefer. Surveys conducted by epidemiologists are run along essentially the same lines: a representative sample of subjects (or patients) is interviewed, examined, or otherwise studied to gain answers to a specific clinical question. In cross sectional surveys, data are collected at a single timepoint but may refer retrospectively to health experiences in the past, such as, for example, the study of patients' casenotes to see how often their blood pressure has been recorded in the past five years.

Clinical questions that should be examined by a cross sectional survey include:

- What is the "normal" height of a 3 year old child? (This, like other questions about the range of normality, can be answered simply by measuring the height of enough healthy 3 year olds. But such an exercise does not answer the related clinical question "When should an unusually short child be investigated for disease?" because, as in almost all biological measurements, the physiological (normal) overlaps with the pathological (abnormal). This problem is discussed further in section 7.4)

- What do psychiatric nurses believe about the value of electroconvulsive therapy (ECT) in the treatment of severe depression?

- Is it true that "half of all cases of diabetes are undiagnosed"? (This an example of the more general question, "What is the prevalence (proportion of people with the condition) of this disease in this community?" The only way of finding the answer is to do the definitive diagnostic test on a representative sample of the population.)

## 3.7 Case reports

A case report describes the medical history of a single patient in the form of a story ("Mrs B is a 54 year old secretary who developed chest pain in June 1995..."). Case reports are often run together to form a *case series,* in which the medical histories of more than one patient with a particular condition are described to illustrate an aspect of the condition, the treatment, or, most commonly these days, an adverse reaction to medication.

Although this type of research is traditionally considered to be relatively weak scientific evidence (see section 3.8), a great deal of information can be conveyed in a case report that would be lost in a clinical trial or survey (see chapter 11). In addition, case reports are immediately understandable by non-academic clinicians and by the lay public. They can, if necessary, be written up and published within days, which gives them a definite edge over meta-analyses (whose gestation can run into years) or clinical trials (several months). There is certainly a vocal pressure group within the medical profession calling for the reinstatement of the humble case report as a useful and valid contribution to medical science[39].

Clinical situations in which a case report or case series is an appropriate type of study include:

● A doctor notices that two newborn babies in his hospital have absent limbs (phocomelia). Both mothers had taken a new drug (thalidomide) in early pregnancy. The doctor wishes to alert his colleagues worldwide to the possibility of drug related damage as quickly as possible[40]. (Anyone who thinks "quick and dirty" case reports are never scientifically justified should remember this example)

● A patient who has taken two different drugs, terfenadine (for hay fever) and itraconazole (for fungal infection) with no side effects in the past takes than concurrently (that is, both at the same time) and develops a life threatening heart rhythm disturbance. The doctors treating him suspect that the two drugs are interacting[41].

## 3.8 The traditional hierarchy of evidence

Standard notation for the relative weight carried by the different types of primary study when decisions are made about clinical interventions (the "hierarchy of evidence") puts them in the following order[42]:

1 Systematic reviews and meta-analyses (see chapter 8)

2 Randomised controlled trials with definitive results (that is, a result with confidence intervals that do not overlap the threshold clinically significant effect; see section 5.5)

3 Randomised controlled trials with non-definitive results (that is, a point estimate that suggests a clinically significant effect but with confidence intervals overlapping the threshold for this effect; see section 5.5)

4 Cohort studies

5 Case-control studies

6 Cross sectional surveys

7 Case reports.

The pinnacle of the hierarchy is, quite properly, reserved for secondary research papers, in which all the primary studies on a particular subject have been hunted out and critically appraised according to rigorous criteria (see chapter 8). Note, however, that not even the most hard line protagonist of evidence based medicine would place a sloppy meta-analysis or a randomised controlled trial that was seriously methodologically flawed above a large, well designed cohort study. And as chapter 11 shows, many important and valid studies in the field of qualitative research do not feature in this particular hierarchy of evidence at all. In other words, evaluating the potential contribution of a particular study to medical science requires considerably more effort than is needed to check off its basic design against the seven point scale above.

## 3.9 A note on ethical considerations

When I was a junior doctor, I got a job in a world renowned teaching hospital. One of my humble tasks was seeing the geriatric (elderly) patients in casualty. I was soon invited out to lunch by two charming registrars, who (I later realised) were seeking my help with their research. In return for getting my name on the paper, I was to take a rectal biopsy (that is, cut out a small piece of tissue from the rectum) on any patient over the age of 90 who had constipation. I asked for a copy of the consent form that patients would be asked to sign. When they assured me that the average 90 year old would hardly notice the procedure, I smelt a rat and refused to cooperate with their project.

I was naïvely unaware of the seriousness of the offence being planned by these doctors. Doing *any* research, particularly that which entails invasive procedures, on vulnerable and sick patients without full consideration of ethical issues is both a criminal offence and potential grounds for a doctor to be "struck off" the medical register. Getting ethical approval for one's research study can be an enormous bureaucratic hurdle[43], but it is nevertheless a legal requirement (and one which is, sadly, sometimes ignored in research into elderly people and those with learning difficulties[44]). Most editors routinely refuse to publish research that has not been approved by the local research ethics committee, but if you are in doubt about a paper's status, there is nothing to stop you writing to ask the authors for copies of relevant documents.

Note, however, that this hand can be overplayed[43]. Research ethics committees frequently deem research proposals unethical, yet it could be argued that in areas of genuine clinical uncertainty the only ethical option is to allow the informed patient the opportunity to help reduce that uncertainty. The randomised trial that showed that neural tube defects could be prevented by giving folic acid supplements to the mother in early pregnancy[45] is said to have been held back for years because of ethics committee resistance.

[1]  Altman DG. The scandal of poor medical research. *BMJ* 1994; **308**: 283-4.
[2]  Lock S. A question of balance: editorial peer review in medicine. London: BMJ Publishing, 1986.
[3]  Sackett DL, Haynes RB, Guyatt GH, *et al. Clinical epidemiology—a basic science for clinical medicine.* London: Little, Brown, 1991.
[4]  Sackett DL, Richardson WS, Rosenberg WMC, *et al. Evidence-based medicine: how to practice and teach EBM.* London: Churchill-Livingstone, 1996.
[5]  Crombie IM. *The pocket guide to critical appraisal.* London: BMJ Publishing, 1996.
[6]  Fletcher RH, Fletcher SW, Wagner EH. *Clinical epidemiology: the essentials.* 3rd edition. Baltimore: Williams and Williams, 1996.
[7]  Rose G, Barker DJP. *Epidemiology for the uninitiated.* 3rd ed. London: BMJ Publishing, 1993.
[8]  Oxman AD, Sackett DS, Guyatt GH. Users' guides to the medical literature. I. How to get started. *JAMA* 1993; **270**: 2093-5.
[9]  Guyatt GH, Sackett DL, Cook DJ. Users' guides to the medical literature. II. How to use an article about therapy or prevention. A. Are the results of the study valid? *JAMA* 1993; **270**: 2598-601.

10 Guyatt GH, Sackett DL, Cook DJ. Users' guides to the medical literature. II. How to use an article about therapy or prevention. B. What were the results and will they help me in caring for my patients? *JAMA* 1994; **271**: 59-63.

11 Jaeschke R, Guyatt G, Sackett DL. Users' guides to the medical literature. III. How to use an article about a diagnostic test. A. Are the results of the study valid? *JAMA* 1994; **271**: 389-91.

12 Jaeschke R, Guyatt G, Sackett DL. Users' guides to the medical literature. III. How to use an article about a diagnostic test. B. What were the results and will they help me in caring for my patients? *JAMA* 1994; **271**: 703-7.

13 Levine M, Walter S, Lee H, *et al.* Users' guides to the medical literature. IV. How to use an article about harm. *JAMA* 1994; **271**: 1615-9.

14 Laupacis A, Wells G, Richardson WS, *et al.* Users' guides to the medical literature. V. How to use an article about prognosis. *JAMA* 1994; **271**: 234-7.

15 Oxman AD, Cox DJ, Guyatt GH. Users' guides to the medical literature. VI. How to use an overview. *JAMA* 1994; **272**: 1367-71.

16 Richardson WS, Detsky AS. Users' guides to the medical literature. VII. How to use a clinical decision analysis. A. Are the results of the study valid? *JAMA* 1995; **273**: 1292-5.

17 Richardson WS, Detsky AS. Users' guides to the medical literature. VII. How to use a clinical decision analysis. B. What are the results and will they help me in caring for my patients? *JAMA* 1995; **273**: 1610-3.

18 Hayward RSA, Wilson MC, Tunis SR, *et al.* Users' guides to the medical literature. VIII. How to use clinical practice guidelines. A. Are the recommendations valid? *JAMA* 1995; **274**: 570-4.

19 Wilson MC, Hayward RS, Tunis SR, *et al.* Users' guides to the medical literature. VIII. How to use clinical practice guidelines. B. Will the recommendations help me in caring for my patients? *JAMA* 1995; **274**: 1630-2.

20 McMaster University Health Sciences Centre. How to read clinical journals. VII. To understand an economic evaluation: A. *Can Med Assoc J* 1984; **130**: 1428-34.

21 McMaster University Health Sciences Centre. How to read clinical journals. VII. To understand an economic evaluation: B. *Can Med Assoc J* 1984; **130**: 1542-9.

22 Popper K. *Conjectures and refutations: the growth of scientific knowledge.* New York: Routledge and Kegan Paul, 1963.

23 ISIS-2 Collaborative Group. Randomised trial of intravenous streptokinase, aspirin, both, or neither among 17 187 cases of suspected acute myocardial infarction: ISIS-2. Lancet 1988; II: 349-60.

24 Thornton JG, Lilford RJ, Johnson N. Decision analysis in medicine. *BMJ* 1992; **304**: 1099-103.

25 Thornton JG, Lilford RJ. Decision analysis for medical managers. *BMJ* 1995; **310**: 791-4.

26 Dowie J. 'Evidence-based', 'cost-effective', and 'preference-driven' medicine. *J Health Serv Res Pol* 1996; **1**: 104-13.

27 Stewart LA, Parmar MKB. Bias in the analysis and reporting of randomized controlled trials. *Int J Health Technol Assess* 1996; **12**: 264-75.

28 Bero LA, Rennie D. Influences on the quality of published drug studies. *Int J Health Technol Assess* 1996; **12**: 209-37.

29 MacIntyre IMC. Tribulations for clinical trials. Poor recruitment is hampering research. *BMJ* 1991; **302**: 1099-100.

30 Easterbrook PJ, Berlin JA, Gopalan R, *et al.* Publication bias in clinical research. *Lancet* 1991; **337**: 867-72.

31 Lumley J, Bastian H. Competing or complementary: ethical considerations and the quality of randomised trials. *Int J Health Technol Assess* 1996; **12**: 1247-63.

[32] Britten N, Jones R, Murphy E, et al. Qualitative research methods in general practice and primary care. *Fam Pract* 1995; **12**: 104-14.

[33] Mays N, Pope C, eds. *Qualitative research in health care*. London: BMJ Publishing, 1996.

[34] Altman D. Better reporting of randomised controlled trials: the CONSORT statement. *BMJ* 1996; **313**: 570-1.

[35] Doll R, Hill AB. Mortality in relation to smoking: ten years' observations of British doctors. *BMJ* 1964; **i**: 1399-414, 1460-7.

[36] Doll R, Peto R. Mortality in relation to smoking: 20 years' observations on British doctors. *BMJ* 1976; **ii**: 1525-36.

[37] Doll R, Peto R, Wheatley K, et al. Mortality in relation to smoking: 40 years' observations on male British doctors. *BMJ* 1994; **309**: 901-11.

[38] Guillebaud J. *The Pill*. 4th ed. Oxford: Oxford University Press, 1991.

[39] Macnaughton J. Anecdotes and empiricism. *Br J Gen Pract* 1995; **45**: 571-2.

[40] McBride WG. Thalidomide and congenital abnormalities. *Lancet* 1961; **ii**: 1358.

[41] Pohjola-Sintonen S, Viitasalo M, Toivonen L, et al. Itraconazole prevents terfenadine metabolism and increases the risk of torsades de pointes ventricular tachycardia. *Eur J Clin Pharm* 1993; **45**: 191-3.

[42] Guyatt GH, Sackett DL, Sinclair JC, et al. Users' guides to the medical literature. IX. A method for grading health care recommendations. *JAMA* 1995; **274**: 1800-4.

[43] Middle C, Johnson A, Petty T, et al. Ethics approval for a national postal survey: recent experience. *BMJ* 1995; **311**: 659-60.

[44] Olde Rickert MGM, ten Have HAMJ, Hoefnagels WHL. Informed consent in biomedical studies on aging: survey of four journals. *BMJ* 1996; **313**: 1117.

[45] MRC Vitamin Research Group. Prevention of neural tube defects. Results of the MRC vitamin study. *Lancet* 1991; **338**: 131-7.

# Chapter 4: Assessing methodological quality

As I argued in section 3.1, a paper will sink or swim on the strength of its methods section. This chapter considers five essential questions that should form the basis of your decision to "bin it", suspend judgment, or use it to influence your practice: was the study original, whom is it about, was it well designed, was systematic bias avoided (that is, was the study adequately "controlled"), and was it large enough and continued for long enough to make the results credible? These questions are considered in turn below.

## 4.1 Was the study original?

There is, in theory, no point in testing a scientific question that someone else has already proved one way or the other. But in real life, science is seldom so cut and dried. Only a tiny proportion of medical research breaks entirely new ground, and an equally tiny proportion repeats exactly the steps of previous workers. The vast majority of research studies will tell us (if they are methodologically sound) that a particular hypothesis is slightly more or less likely to be correct than it was before we added our piece to the wider jigsaw. Hence, it may be perfectly valid to do a study that is, on the face of it, "unoriginal". Indeed, the whole science of meta-analysis depends on there being more than one study in the literature that has examined the same question in pretty much the same way.

The practical question to ask, then, about a new piece of research is not "has anyone ever done a similar study before?" but "does this new research add to the literature in any way?" For example,

● Is this study bigger, continued for longer, or otherwise more substantial than the previous one(s)?

● Is the methodology of this study any more rigorous (in particular, does it cover any specific methodological criticisms of previous studies)?

● Will the numerical results of this study add significantly to a meta-analysis of previous studies?

● Is the population studied different in any way (for example, has the study looked at different ethnic groups, ages, or gender than previous studies)?

● Is the clinical issue examined of sufficient importance and does there exist sufficient doubt in the minds of the public or key decision makers to make new evidence "politically" desirable even when it is not strictly scientifically necessary?

## 4.2 Who is the study about?

One of the first papers that ever caught my eye was entitled "But will it help *my* patients with myocardial infarction?[1]. I don't remember the details of the article, but it opened my eyes to the fact that research on someone else's patients may not have a take home message for my own practice. This is not mere xenophobia. The main reasons why the subjects (or patients) in a clinical trial or survey might differ from patients in "real life" are as follows:

● They were more, or less, ill than the patients you see

● They were from a different ethnic group, or lived a different lifestyle, from your own patients

● They received more (or different) attention during the study than you could ever hope to give your patients

● Unlike most real life patients, they had nothing wrong with them apart from the condition being studied

● None of them smoked, drank alcohol, or were taking the contraceptive pill.

Hence, before swallowing the results of any paper whole, ask yourself the following questions:

*How were the subjects recruited?*—If you wanted to do a questionnaire survey of the views of users of the hospital casualty department you could recruit respondents by putting an ad in the local newspaper. However, this method would be a good example of *recruitment bias* as the sample you obtain would be skewed in favour of users who were highly motivated and liked to read newspapers. You would, of course, be better to issue a questionnaire to every user (or to a one in 10 sample of users) who turned up on a particular day.

*Who was included in the study?*—Many trials in the UK routinely exclude patients with coexisting illness, those who do not speak English, those taking certain other medication, and the illiterate. This approach may be scientifically "clean" but as clinical trial results will be used to guide practice in relation to wider patient groups, it is not necessarily all that logical[2]. The results of pharmacokinetic studies of new drugs in 23 year old healthy male volunteers will clearly not be applicable to the average elderly woman. This issue, which has been a bugbear of some doctors for some time[3], has recently been taken up by the patients themselves, most notably in the plea from patient support groups for a broadening of inclusion criteria in trials of drugs for the treatment of AIDS.

*Who was excluded from the study?*—For example, a randomised controlled trial may be restricted to patients with moderate or severe forms of a disease such as heart failure—a policy that could lead to false conclusions about the treatment of *mild* heart failure. This has important practical implications when clinical trials performed on hospital outpatients are used to dictate "best practice" in primary care, where the spectrum of disease is generally milder.

*Were the subjects studied in "real life" circumstances?*—For example, were they admitted to hospital purely for observation? Did they receive lengthy and detailed explanations of the potential benefits of the intervention? Were they given the telephone number of a key research worker? Did the company who funded the research provide new equipment that would not be available to the ordinary clinician? These factors would not, of course, invalidate the study itself, but they may cast doubt on the applicability of its findings to your own practice.

## 4.3 Was the design of the study sensible?

Although the terminology of research trial design can be forbidding, much of what is grandly termed "critical appraisal" is plain common sense. Personally, I assess the basic design of a clinical trial through two questions:

*What specific intervention or other manoeuvre was being considered and what was it being compared with?*—This is one of the most fundamental questions in appraising any paper. It is tempting to take published statements at face value, but remember that authors commonly misrepresent (usually subconsciously rather than deliberately) what they actually did, and overestimate its originality and potential importance. In the examples in box 4.1, I have used hypothetical statements so as not to cause offence, but they are all based on similar mistakes seen in print.

*What outcome was measured and how?*—If you had an incurable disease for which a pharmaceutical company claimed to have produced a new wonder drug you would measure the efficacy of the drug in terms of whether it made you live longer (and, perhaps, whether life was *worth* living given your condition and any side effects of the medication). You would not be too interested in the levels of some obscure enzyme in your blood that the manufacturer assured you were a reliable indicator of your chances of survival. The use of such *surrogate end points* is discussed further in section 6.3.

The measurement of symptomatic (for example, pain), functional (for example, mobility), psychological (for example, anxiety), or social (for example, inconvenience) effects of an intervention is fraught with even more problems. The methodology of developing, administering, and interpreting such "soft" outcome measures is beyond the scope of this book. But in general, you should always look for evidence in the paper that the outcome measure has been objectively validated—that is, that someone has

# Box 4.1 Examples of problematic descriptions in the methods section of papers

| What the authors said | What they should have said (or should have done) | An example of |
|---|---|---|
| "We measured how often GPs ask patients whether they smoke" | "We looked in patients' medical records and counted how many had had their smoking status recorded" | Assumption that medical records are 100% accurate |
| "We measured how doctors treat low back pain" | "We measured what doctors say they do when faced with a patient with low back pain" | Assumption that what doctors say they do reflects what they actually do |
| "We compared a nicotine replacement patch with placebo" | "Subjects in the intervention group were asked to apply a patch containing 15 mg nicotine twice daily; those in the control group received identical looking patches" | Failure to state dose of drug or nature of placebo |
| "We asked 100 teenagers to participate in our survey of sexual attitudes" | "We approached 147 white American teenagers aged 12-18 (85 males) at a summer camp; 100 of them (31 males) agreed to participate" | Failure to give sufficient information about subjects (note in this example the figures indicate a recruitment bias towards females) |
| "We randomised patients to either 'individual care plan' or 'usual care'" | "The intervention group were offered an individual care plan consisting of...; control patients were offered..." | Failure to give sufficient information about intervention (enough information should be given to allow the study to be repeated by other workers) |
| "To assess the value of an educational leaflet, we gave the intervention group a leaflet and a telephone helpline number. Controls received neither" | If the study is purely to assess the value of the leaflet, both groups should have got the helpline number | Failure to treat groups equally apart form the specific intervention |
| "We measured the use of vitamin C in the prevention of the common cold" | A systematic literature search would have found numerous previous studies on this subject (see section 8.1) | Unoriginal study |

demonstrated that the scale of anxiety, pain, and so on used in this study has previously been shown to measure what it purports to measure and that changes in this outcome measure adequately reflect changes in the status of the patient. Remember that what is important in the eyes of the doctor may not be valued so highly by the patient and vice versa[5].

## 4.4 Was systematic bias avoided or minimised?

Systematic bias is defined by epidemiologists Geoffrey Rose and David Barker as anything that erroneously influences the conclusions about groups and distorts comparisons[6]. Whether the design of a study is a randomised controlled trial, a non-randomised comparative trial, a cohort study, or a case-control study, the aim should be for the groups being compared to be as like one another as possible except for the particular difference being examined. They should, as far as possible, receive the same explanations, have the same contacts with health professionals, and be assessed the same number of times with the same outcome measures. Different study designs call for different steps to reduce systematic bias.

*Randomised controlled trials*

In a randomised controlled trial, systematic bias is (in theory) avoided by the selection of a sample of participants from a particular population and allocation of them randomly to the different groups. Section 3.3 describes some ways in which bias can creep into even this gold standard of clinical trial design, and figure 4.1 summarises particular sources to check for.

*Non-randomised comparative trials*

I recently chaired a seminar in which a multidisciplinary group of students from the medical, nursing, pharmacy, and allied professions were presenting the results of several in house research studies. All but one of the studies presented were of comparative but non-randomised design—that is, one group of patients (say, hospital outpatients with asthma) had received one intervention (say, an educational leaflet) while another group (say, patients with asthma attending GP surgeries) had received another intervention

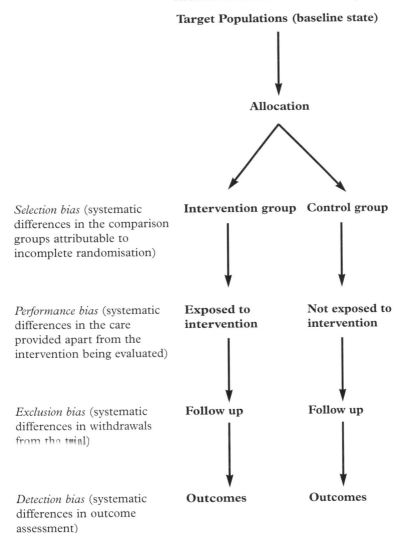

Figure 4.1 Sources of bias to check for in a randomised controlled trial

(say, group educational sessions). I was surprised how many of the presenters believed that their study was, or was equivalent to, a randomised controlled trial. In other words, these commendably enthusiastic and committed young researchers were blind to the most obvious bias of all: they were comparing two groups that had inherent, self selected differences even before the intervention was applied (as well as having all the additional potential sources of bias listed in figure 4.1 for randomised controlled trials).

As a general rule, if the paper you are looking at is a non-randomised controlled clinical trial you must use your common sense to decide if the baseline differences between the intervention and control groups are likely to have been so great as to invalidate any differences ascribed to the effects of the intervention. This is, in fact, almost always the case[7] [8]. Sometimes, the authors of such a paper will list the important features of each group (such as mean age, sex ratio, markers of disease severity, and so on) in a table to allow you to compare these differences yourself.

### Cohort studies

The selection of a comparable control group is one of the most difficult decisions facing the authors of an observational (cohort or case-control) study. Few, if any, cohort studies, for example, succeed in identifying two groups of subjects who are equal in age, sex ratio, socioeconomic status, presence of coexisting illness, and so on, with the single difference being their exposure to the agent being studied. In practice, much of the "controlling" in cohort studies occurs at the analysis stage, where complex statistical adjustment is made for baseline differences in key variables. Unless this is done adequately, statistical tests of probability and confidence intervals (see section 5.5) will be dangerously misleading[9].

This problem is illustrated by the various cohort studies on the risks and benefits of alcohol, which have consistently demonstrated a "J shaped" relation between alcohol intake and mortality. The best outcome (in terms of premature death) lies with the cohort who are moderate drinkers[10]. Self confessed teetotalers, it seems, are significantly more likely to die young than the average person who drinks three or four drinks a day.

But can we assume that teetotalers are, *on average*, identical to moderate drinkers except for the amount they drink? We certainly can't. As we all know, the teetotal population includes those who have been ordered to give up alcohol on health grounds ("sick quitters"), those who, for health or other reasons, have cut out a host of additional items from their diet and lifestyle, those from certain religious or ethnic groups, which may be under-represented in the other cohorts (notably Muslims and Seventh Day Adventists), and those who drink like fish but choose to lie about it.

The details of how these different features of "teetotalism" were controlled for by the epidemiologists are discussed elsewhere[10]. In summary, even when due allowance is made in the analysis for potential confounding variables in subjects who describe themselves as non-drinkers, these subjects' increased risk of premature mortality seems to remain.

## Case-control studies

In case-control studies (in which, as I explained in section 3.5, the experiences of individuals with and without a particular disease are analysed retrospectively to identify putative causative events), the process that is most open to bias is not the assessment of outcome but the diagnosis of "caseness" and the decision as to *when* the individual became a case.

A good example of this occurred a few years ago when a legal action was brought against the manufacturers of the whooping cough (pertussis) vaccine, which was alleged to have caused neurological damage in a number of infants[11]. To answer the question "Did the vaccine cause brain damage?" a case-control study had been undertaken in which a "case" was defined as an infant who, previously well, had exhibited fits or other signs suggestive of brain damage within one week after receiving the vaccine. A control was an infant of the same age and sex taken from the same immunisation register, who had received immunisation, and who may or may not have developed symptoms at some stage.

New onset of features of brain damage in apparently normal babies is extremely rare, but it does happen, and the link with recent immunisation could conceivably be coincidental. Furthermore, heightened public anxiety about the issue could have biased the recall of parents and health professionals so that infants whose neurological symptoms predated, or occurred some time after, the administration of pertussis vaccine, might be wrongly classified as cases. The judge in the court case ruled that

61

misclassification of three such infants as "cases" rather than controls led to the overestimation of the harm attributable to whooping cough vaccine by a factor of three[11]. Although this ruling has subsequently been challenged, the principle stands— that assignment of "caseness" in a case-control study must be done rigorously and objectively if systematic bias is to be avoided.

## 4.5 Was assessment "blind"?

Even the most rigorous attempt to achieve a comparable control group will be wasted effort if the people who assess outcome (for example, those who judge whether someone is still clinically in heart failure or who say whether an $x$ ray finding has "improved" since the last time) know to which group the patient they are assessing was allocated. If you believe that the evaluation of clinical signs and the interpretation of diagnostic tests such as electrocardiograms and $x$ ray photography is 100% objective you haven't been in the game very long.

The chapter "The Clinical Examination" in Sackett and colleagues' book *Clinical epidemiology: a basic science for clinical medicine* provides substantial evidence that when they examine patients, doctors find what they expect and hope to find[12]. It is rare indeed for two competent clinicians to reach agreement beyond what would be expected by chance in more than two cases in every three for any given aspect of the physical examination or interpretation of any diagnostic test.

The level of agreement beyond chance between two observers can be expressed mathematically as the $\kappa$ (Kappa) score, with a score of 1.0 indicating perfect agreement. $\kappa$ scores for specialists in the field assessing the height of a patient's jugular venous pressure, classifying diabetic retinopathy from retinal photographs, and interpreting a mammogram $x$ ray picture, were, respectively, 0.42, 0.55, and 0.67[12].

The above digression into clinical disagreement should have persuaded you that efforts to keep assessors "blind" to the group allocation of their patients are far from superfluous. If, for example, I knew that a patient had been randomised to an active drug to lower blood pressure rather than to a placebo, I might be more likely to recheck a reading that was surprisingly high. This is an example of *performance bias* which, along with other pitfalls for the unblinded assessor, are listed in figure 4.1.

An excellent example of controlling for bias by adequate "blinding" was published in the *Lancet* recently[13]. Majeed and colleagues performed a randomised controlled trial that demonstrated, in contrast with the findings of several previous studies, that the recovery time (days in hospital, days off work, and time to resume full activity) after laparoscopic removal of the gall bladder (the "keyhole surgery" approach) was no quicker than that associated with traditional open operation. The discrepancy between this trial and its predecessors may have been due to Majeed and colleagues' meticulous attempt to reduce bias (see figure 4.1). The patients were not randomised until after induction of general anaesthesia. Neither the patients nor their carers were aware of which operation had been done as all patients left the operating theatre with identical dressings (complete with blood stains). These findings challenge previous authors to ask themselves whether it was expectation bias (see section 7.3) rather than swifter recovery that spurred doctors to discharge the laparoscopic surgery group earlier.

## 4.6 Were preliminary statistical questions dealt with?

As a non-statistician, I tend only to look for three numbers in the methods section of a paper:

● The size of the sample

● The duration of follow up

● The completeness of follow up

*Sample size*

One crucial prerequisite before embarking on a clinical trial is to perform a sample size ("power") calculation. In the words of statistician Douglas Altman, a trial should be big enough to have a high chance of detecting, as statistically significant, a worthwhile effect if it exists, and thus to be reasonably sure that no benefit exists if it is not found in the trial[14].

To calculate sample size, the clinician must decide two things:

● What level of difference between the two groups would constitute a *clinically significant* effect. Note that this may not be the same as a statistically significant effect. You could administer a new drug that lowered blood pressure by around 10 mm Hg, and the effect would be a statistically significant lowering of the chances of developing stroke (that is, the odds are less than 1 in 20 that the reduced incidence occurred by chance)[15]. However, if the people being asked to take this drug had only mildly raised blood pressure and no other major risk factors for stroke (that is, they were relatively young, not diabetic, had normal cholesterol concentrations, and so on) this amount of difference would prevent only around one stroke in every 850 patients treated[16]—a *clinical* difference in risk that many patients would classify as not worth the effort of taking the tablets.

● What the mean and the standard deviation (abbreviated SD; see section 5.2) of the principal outcome variable is.

By using a statistical nomogram[14], the authors can then, *before the trial begins,* work out how large a sample they will need to have a moderate, high, or very high chance of detecting a true difference between the groups. The likelihood of detecting a true difference is known as the *power* of the study. It is common for studies to stipulate a power of between 80% and 90%. Hence, when reading a paper about a randomised controlled trial, you should look for a sentence that reads something like this (which is taken from Majeed and colleagues' cholecystectomy paper described above):

> "For a 90% chance of detecting a difference of one night's stay in hospital using the Mann-Whitney U-test [see table 5.1], 100 patients were needed in each group (assuming SD of 2 nights). This gives a power greater than 90% for detecting a difference in operating times of 15 minutes, assuming a SD of 20 minutes".[13]

If the paper you are reading does not give a sample size calculation *and* it seems to show that there is no difference between the intervention and control arms of the trial, you should extract from the paper (or directly from the authors) the size of the sample and the length of follow up and do the calculation yourself. Underpowered studies are ubiquitous in the medical literature, usually because the authors found it harder than they anticipated to recruit their subjects. Such studies typically lead to a type II or $\beta$ error—that is, the erroneous conclusion that an intervention has no effect. (In contrast, the rarer type I or $\alpha$ error is the conclusion that a difference is significant when in fact it is due to sampling error.)

*Duration of follow up*

Even if the sample size itself was adequate, a study must be continued for long enough for the effect of the intervention to be reflected in the outcome variable. If the authors were looking at the effect of a new painkiller on the degree of postoperative pain, their study may have needed a follow up period of only 48 hours. On the other hand, if they were looking at the effect of nutritional supplementation in the preschool years on final adult height, follow up should have been measured in decades.

Even if the intervention has demonstrated a significant difference between the groups after, say, six months, that difference may not be sustained. As many dieters know from bitter experience, strategies to reduce obesity often show dramatic results after two or three weeks but if follow up is continued for a year or more the unfortunate subjects have (more often than not) put most of the weight back on.

*Completeness of follow up*

It has been shown repeatedly that subjects who withdraw from ("drop out of") research studies are less likely to have taken their tablets as directed, more likely to have missed their interim check ups, and more likely to have experienced side effects on any medication than those who do not withdraw[12]. People who fail to complete questionnaires may feel differently about the issue (and probably less strongly) than those who send them back by return of post. People on a weight reducing programme are more likely to continue coming back if they are actually losing weight.

The reasons why patients withdraw from clinical trials include the following.

● Incorrect entry of patient into trial (that is, researcher discovers during the trial that the patient should not have been randomised in the first place because he or she did not fulfil the entry criteria)

● Suspected adverse reaction to the trial drug. Note that you should never look at the "adverse reaction" rate in the intervention group without comparing it with that on placebo. Inert tablets bring people out in a rash surprising often

● Loss of patient motivation ("I don't want to take these tablets any more")

● Withdrawal by clinician for clinical reasons (for example, concurrent illness, pregnancy)

● Loss to follow up (for example, patient moves away)

● Death. Clearly, patients who die will not attend for their outpatient appointments, so unless specifically accounted for they might be misclassified as "drop outs". This is one reason why studies with a low follow up rate (say below 70%) are generally considered invalid.

Simply ignoring everyone who has withdrawn from a clinical trial will bias the results, usually in favour of the intervention. It is, therefore, standard practice to analyse the results of comparative studies on an *intent to treat* basis[17]. This means that all data on patients originally allocated to the intervention arm of the study, including those who withdrew before the trial finished, those who did not take their tablets, and even those who subsequently received the control intervention for whatever reason, should be analysed along with data on the patients who followed the protocol throughout. Conversely, withdrawals from the placebo arm of the study should be analysed with those who faithfully took their placebo. If you look hard enough in a paper, you will usually find the sentence, "results were analysed on an intent to treat basis", but you should not be reassured until you have checked and confirmed the figures yourself.

There are, in fact, a few situations when intent to treat analysis is, rightly, not used. The most common is the *efficacy analysis,* which is to explain the effects of the intervention itself and is therefore of the treatment actually received. But even if the subjects in an efficacy analysis are part of a randomised controlled trial, for the purposes of the analysis they effectively constitute a cohort study (see section 3.4).

## 4.7 Summing up

Having worked through the Methods section, you should be able to tell yourself in a short paragraph what sort of study was performed, on how many subjects, where the subjects came from, what treatment or other intervention was offered, how long the follow up period was (or, if a survey, what the response rate was), and what outcome measure(s) were used. You should also, at this stage, identify what statistical tests, if any, were used to analyse the results (see chapter 5). If you are clear about these things before reading the rest of the paper, you will find the results easier to understand, interpret, and, if appropriate, reject. You should be able to come up with descriptions such as:

"This paper describes an unblinded randomised trial, concerned with therapy, in 267 hospital outpatients aged between 58 and 93 years, in which four layer compression bandaging was compared with standard single layer dressings in the management of uncomplicated venous leg ulcers. Follow up was six months. Percentage healing of the ulcer was measured from baseline in terms of the surface area of a tracing of the wound taken by the district nurse and calculated by a computer scanning device. Results were analysed with the Wilcoxon matched pairs test."

"This is a questionnaire survey of 963 general practitioners randomly selected from throughout the UK, in which they were asked their year of graduation from medical school and the level at which they would begin treatment for essential hypertension. Response options on the structured questionnaire were '90-99 mm Hg', '100-109 mm Hg', and '110 mm Hg or greater'. Results were analysed with a $\chi^2$ test on a 3 × 2 table to see whether the threshold for treating hypertension was related to whether the doctor graduated from medical school before or after 1975."

"This is a case report of a single patient with a suspected fatal adverse drug reaction to the newly released hypnotic drug Sleepol."

When you have had a little practice in looking at the methods section of research papers along the lines suggested in this chapter, you will find that it is only a short step to start using the checklists in appendix A or the more comprehensive "Users' guides to the medical literature" referenced in chapter 3. I will return to many of the issues discussed here in chapter 6, in relation to evaluating papers on drug trials.

[1] Mitchell JR. But will it help *my* patients with myocardial infarction? *BMJ* 1982; **285**: 1140-8.
[2] Bero LA, Rennie D. Influences on the quality of published drug studies. *Int J Health Technol Assess* 1996; **12**: 209-37.
[3] Buyse ME. The case for loose inclusion criteria in clinical trials. *Acta Chirurgica Belgica* 1990; **90**: 129-31.
[4] Phillips AN, Davey Smith G, Johnson MA. Will we ever know how to treat HIV infection? *BMJ* 1996; **313**: 608-10.
[5] Dunning M, Needham G. *But will it work doctor? Report of conference held in Northampton, 22nd and 23rd May 1996.* London: Kings Fund, 1997.
[6] Rose G, Barker DJP. *Epidemiology for the uninitiated.* 3rd ed. London: BMJ Publishing, 1994.
[7] Chalmers TC, Celano P, Sacks HS, *et al.* Bias in treatment assignment in controlled clinical trials. *N Engl J Med* 1983; **309**: 1358-61.

8  Colditz GA, Miller JA, Mosteller JF. How study design affects outcome in comparisons of therapy. I. Medical. *Stat Med* 1989: **8**: 441-54.

9  Brennan P, Croft P. Interpreting the results of observational research: chance is not such a fine thing. *BMJ* 1994; **309**: 727-30.

10 Maclure M. Demonstration of deductive meta-analysis: alcohol intake and risk of myocardial infarction. *Epidemiol Rev* 1993; **15**: 328-51.

11 Bowie C. Lessons from the pertussis vaccine trial. *Lancet* 1990; **335**: 397-9.

12 Sackett DL, Haynes RB, Guyatt GH, *et al. Clinical epidemiology - a basic science for clinical medicine.* London: Little, Brown, 1991: 19-49.

13 Majeed AW, Troy G, Nicholl JP, *et al.* Randomised, prospective, single-blind comparison of laparoscopic versus small-incision cholecystectomy. *Lancet* 1996; **347**: 989-94.

14 Altman D. *Practical statistics for medical research.* London: Chapman & Hall, 1991. (The nomogram for calculating sample size or power is on page 456.)

15 Medical Research Council Working Party. MRC trial of mild hypertension: principal results. *BMJ* 1985; **291**: 97-104.

16 MacMahon S, Rogers A. The effects of antihypertensive treatment on vascular disease: re-appraisal of the evidence in 1993. *J Vascular Med Biol* 1993; **4**: 265-71.

17 Stewart LA, Parmar MKB. Bias in the analysis and reporting of randomized controlled trials. *Int J Health Technol Assess* 1996; **12**: 264-75.

# Chapter 5: Statistics for the non-statistician

## 5.1 How can non-statisticians evaluate statistical tests?

In this age when medicine leans increasingly on mathematics, no clinician can afford to leave the statistical aspects of a paper entirely to the "experts". If, like me, you believe yourself to be innumerate, remember that you do not need to be able to build a car to drive one. What you do need to know about statistical tests is which is the best test to use for common problems. You need to be able to describe *in words* what the test does and in what circumstances it becomes invalid or inappropriate. Box 5.1 shows some commonly used "tricks of the trade", which all of us need to be alert to (in our own as well as other people's practice).

I have found that one of the easiest ways to impress my colleagues is to let slip a comment such as: "Ah, I see these authors have performed a one tailed $F$ test. I would have thought a two tailed test would have been more appropriate in these circumstances". As you will see from the notes below, you do not need to be able to perform the $F$ test yourself to come up with comments like this, but you do need to understand what its tails mean.

The summary checklist in appendix A, explained in detail in the sections below, constitutes my own method for assessing the adequacy of a statistical analysis, which some readers will find too simplistic. If you do, please skip this section and turn either to a more comprehensive presentation for the non-statistician: the "Basic statistics for clinicians" series in the *Canadian Medical*

---

## Box 5.1 Ten ways to cheat on statistical tests when writing up results

- Throw all your data into a computer and report as significant any relation where "P <0.05" (see p 80)
- If baseline differences between the groups favour the intervention group, remember not to adjust for them (see p 71)
- Do not test your data to see if they are normally distributed. If you do, you might get stuck with non-parametric tests, which aren't as much fun (see p 72)
- Ignore all withdrawals ("drop outs") and non-responders so the analysis concerns only subjects who fully complied with treatment (see p 65)
- Always assume that you can plot one set of data against another and calculate an "r value" (Pearson correlation coefficient) (see p 78) and that a "significant" r value proves causation (see p 80)
- If outliers (points that lie a long way from the others on your graph) are messing up your calculations, just rub them out. But if outliers are helping your case, even if they seem to be spurious results, leave then in (see p 76)
- If the confidence intervals of your result overlap zero difference between the groups, leave them out of your report. Better still, mention them briefly in the text but don't draw them in on the graph and ignore them when drawing your conclusions (see p 81)
- If the difference between two groups becomes significant four and a half months into a six month trial, stop the trial and start writing up. Alternatively if at six months the results are "nearly significant" extend the trial for another three weeks (see p 75)
- If your results prove uninteresting, ask the computer to go back and see if any particular subgroups behaved differently. You might find that your intervention worked after all in Chinese women aged 52 to 61 (see p 75)
- If analysing your data the way you plan to does not give the result you wanted, run the figures through a selection of other tests (see p 75)

---

*Association Journal*[1-4] or to a more mainstream statistical textbook[5]. If, on the other hand, you find statistics impossibly difficult, take these points one at a time and return to read the next point only when you feel comfortable with the previous ones. None of the points presupposes a detailed knowledge of the actual calculations involved.

The first question to ask, by the way, is, "Have the authors used any statistical tests at all?" If they are presenting numbers and claiming that these numbers mean something without using statistical methods to prove it they are almost certainly skating on thin ice.

## 5.2 Have the authors set the scene correctly?

*Have they determined whether their groups are comparable and, if necessary, adjusted for baseline differences?*

Most comparative clinical trials include either a table or a paragraph in the text showing the baseline characteristics of the groups being studied. Such a table should demonstrate that both the intervention and control groups are similar in terms of age and sex distribution and key prognostic variables (such as the average size of a cancerous lump). If there are important differences in these baseline characteristics, even though these may be due to chance, it can pose a challenge to your interpretation of results. In this situation, you can carry out certain adjustments to try to allow for these differences and hence strengthen your argument. To find out how to make such adjustments, see the section on this topic in Douglas Altman's book *Practical Statistics for Medical Research*[6].

*What sort of data have they got and have they used appropriate statistical tests?*

Numbers are often used to label the properties of things. We can assign a number to represent our height, weight, and so on. For properties like these, the measurements can be treated as actual numbers. We can, for example, calculate the average weight and height of a group of people by averaging the measurements. But consider a different example, in which we use numbers to label the property "city of origin", where 1 = London, 2 = Manchester, 3 = Birmingham, and so on. We could still calculate the average of these numbers for a particular sample of cases, but we would be completely unable to interpret the result. The same would apply if we labelled the property "liking for *x*", with 1 = not at all, 2 = a bit, and 3 = a lot. Again, we could calculate the "average liking" but the numerical result would be uninterpretable unless we knew that the difference between "not at all" and "a bit" was exactly the same as the difference between "a bit" and "a lot".

All statistical tests are either parametric (that is, they assume that the data were sampled from a particular form of distribution, such as a normal distribution) or non-parametric (that is, they do not assume that the data were sampled from a particular type of distribution). In general, parametric tests are more powerful than non-parametric ones and so should be used if at all possible.

Non-parametric tests look at the *rank order* of the values (which one is the smallest, which one comes next, and so on) and ignore the absolute differences between them. As you might imagine, statistical significance is more difficult to demonstrate with non-parametric tests, and this tempts researchers to use statistics such as the correlation coefficient ($r$ value) (see section 5.4) inappropriately. Not only is the $r$ value (parametric) easier to calculate than an equivalent non-parametric statistic such as Spearman's correlation coefficient ($r_s$), but it is also much more likely to give (apparently) significant results. Unfortunately it will also give an entirely spurious and misleading estimate of the significance of the result, unless the data are appropriate to the test being used. More examples of parametric tests and their non-parametric equivalents (if present) are given in table 5.1.

Another consideration is the shape of the distribution from which the data were sampled. When I was at school, my class plotted the amount of pocket money received against the number of children receiving that amount. The results formed a histogram the same shape as figure 5.1—a "normal" distribution. (The term

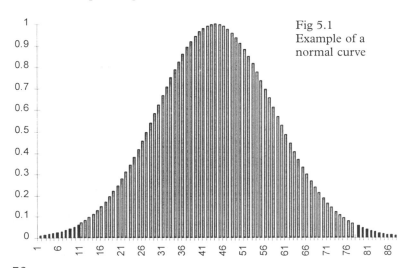

Fig 5.1
Example of a
normal curve

# Table 5.1 Some commonly used statistical tests

| Parametric test | Example of equivalent non-parametric test | Purpose of test | Example |
|---|---|---|---|
| Two sample (unpaired) $t$ test | Mann-Whitney U test | Compares two independent samples drawn from the same population | To compare girls' heights with boys' heights |
| One sample (paired) $t$ test | Wilcoxon matched pairs test | Compares two sets of observations on a single sample | To compare weight of infants before and after a feed |
| One way analysis of variance ($F$ test) using total sum of squares | Kruskall-Wallis analysis of variance by ranks | Effectively, a generalisation of the paired $t$ or Wilcoxon matched pairs test where three or more sets of observations are made on a single sample | To determine whether plasma glucose concentration is higher one hour, two hours, or three hours after a meal |
| Two way analysis of variance | Two way analysis of variance by ranks | As above but tests the influence (and interaction) of two different covariates | In the above example, to determine if the results differ in males and females |
| No direct equivalent | $\chi^2$ Test | Tests the null hypothesis that the proportions of discontinuous variables estimated from two (or more) independent samples are the same | To assess whether acceptance into medical school is more likely if the applicant was born in the UK |
| McNemar's test | No direct equivalent | Tests the null hypothesis that the proportions estimated from a paired sample are the same | To compare the sensitivity and specificity of two different diagnostic tests when applied to the same sample |
| Product moment correlation coefficient (Pearson's $r$) | Spearman's rank correlation coefficient ($r_s$) | Assesses the *strength* of the straight line association between two continuous variables | To assess whether and to what extent plasma HbA1 concentration is related to plasma triglyceride concentration in diabetic patients |
| Regression by least squares method | No direct equivalent | Describes the numerical relation between two quantitative variables, allowing one value to be predicted from the other | To see how peak expiratory flow rate varies with height |
| Multiple regression by least squares method | No direct equivalent | Describes the numerical relation between a dependent variable and several predictor variables (covariates) | To determine whether and to what extent a person's age, body fat, and sodium intake determine their blood pressure |

"normal" refers to the shape of the graph and is used because many biological phenomena show this pattern of distribution.) Some biological variables such as body weight show *skew* distribution, as shown in figures 5.2. (Figure 5.2 in fact shows a negative skew, whereas body weight would be positively skewed.

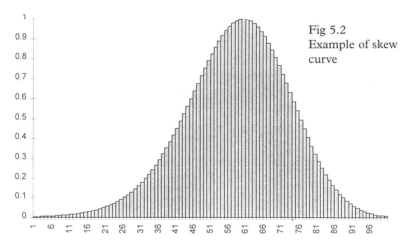

Fig 5.2
Example of skew curve

The average adult male body weight is 70 kg and people exist who are 140 kg but nobody weighs less than nothing, so the graph cannot possibly be symmetrical.)

Non-normal (skewed) data can sometimes be *transformed* to give a normal shape graph by plotting the logarithm of the skewed variable or performing some other mathematical transformation (such as square root or reciprocal). Some data, however, cannot be transformed into a smooth pattern, and the significance of this is discussed below. For a further, very readable, discussion about the normal distribution, see chapter 7 of Martin Bland's book *An Introduction to Medical Statistics*[7].

Deciding whether data are normally distributed is not an academic exercise as it will determine what type of statistical tests to use. For example, linear regression (see section 5.4) will give misleading results unless the points on the scatter graph form a particular distribution about the regression line—that is, the residuals (the perpendicular distance from each point to the line) should themselves be normally distributed. Transforming data to achieve a normal distribution (if this is indeed achievable) is not cheating (it simply ensures that data values are given appropriate emphasis in assessing the overall effect). The use of tests based on the normal distribution to analyse non-normally distributed data is very definitely cheating.

*If the statistical tests in the paper are obscure, why have the authors chosen to use them and have they included a reference?*

There sometimes seems to be an infinite number of possible statistical tests. In fact, most statisticians could survive with a formulary of about a dozen. The rest are small print and should be reserved for special indications. If the paper you are reading seems to describe a standard set of data that has been collected in a standard way but the test used is unpronouncable and not listed in a basic statistics textbook, you should smell a rat. The authors should, in such circumstances, state why they have used this test and give a reference (with page numbers) for a definitive description of it.

*Have the data been analysed according to the original study protocol?*

Even if you are not interested in the statistical justification, common sense should tell you why points 8 and 9 in box 5.1 at the beginning of this chapter amount to serious cheating. If you trawl for long enough you will inevitably find some category of patient that seems to have done particularly well or badly. Each time you look to see if a particular subgroup is different from the rest, however, you greatly increase the likelihood that you will eventually find one that seems to be so, even though the difference is entirely due to chance.

Similarly, if you play coin toss with someone, no matter how far you fall behind, there will come a time when you are one ahead. Most people would agree that to stop the game then would not be a fair way to play. So it is with research. If you make it inevitable that you will (eventually) get an apparently positive result you will also make it inevitable that you will be misleading yourself about the justice of your case[8]. Terminating an intervention trial prematurely for ethical reasons when subjects in one arm are faring particularly badly is different and is discussed elsewhere[8].

Going back and raking over your data to look for "interesting results" (retrospective subgroup analysis) can lead to false conclusions[9]. In an early study on the use of aspirin in the prevention of stroke in predisposed patients, the results showed a significant effect in both sexes combined, and a retrospective subgroup analysis seemed to show that the effect was confined to men[10]. This conclusion led to aspirin being withheld from women for many years until the results of other studies (including a large meta-analysis[11]) showed this subgroup effect to be spurious.

This and other examples are given in a paper by Oxman and Guyatt, "A consumer's guide to subgroup analysis", which reproduces a useful checklist for deciding whether apparent differences in subgroup response are real[12].

## 5.3 Paired data, tails, and outliers

*Were paired tests performed on paired data?*

Students often find it difficult to decide whether to use a paired or unpaired statistical test to analyse their data. There is, in fact, no great mystery about this. If you measure something twice on each subject (for example, lying and standing blood pressure), you will probably be interested not just in the average difference in lying versus standing blood pressure in the entire sample, but in how much each individual's blood pressure changes with position. In this situation, you have what is called "paired" data, because each measurement beforehand is paired with a measurement afterwards.

In this example, it is having the same person on both occasions that makes the pairings, but there are other possibilities (for example, any two measurements of bed occupancy made of the same hospital ward). In these situations, the two sets of values will probably be significantly correlated (for example, my blood pressure next week is likely to be closer to my blood pressure last week than to the blood pressure of a randomly selected adult last week). In other words, we would expect two randomly selected "paired" values to be closer to each other than two randomly selected "unpaired" values. Unless we allow for this by carrying out the appropriate "paired" sample tests, we can end up with a biased estimate of the significance of our results.

*Was a two tailed test performed whenever the effect of an intervention could conceivably be a negative one?*

The concept of a test with tails always has me thinking of devils or snakes, which I guess just reflects my aversion to statistics. In fact, the term tail refers to the extremes of the distribution—the far sides of the bell in figure 5.1. Let's say that that graph represents the distribution of the diastolic blood pressures of a group of individuals, a random sample of whom are about to be put on a low sodium diet. If a low sodium diet has a significant lowering effect on blood pressure, subsequent blood pressure measurements on these subjects would be more likely to lie within the left hand "tail" of the graph. Hence we would analyse the data with statistical tests designed to show whether unusually low readings in this patient sample were likely to have arisen by chance.

But on what grounds may we assume that a low sodium diet could conceivably only put blood pressure down but could never put it *up*? Even if there are valid physiological reasons why that might be the case in this particular example, it is certainly not good science to assume that you always know the *direction* of the effect that your intervention will have. A new drug intended to relieve nausea might actually exacerbate it; and an educational leaflet intended to reduce anxiety might increase it. Hence, your statistical analysis should, in general, test the hypothesis that either high *or* low values in your dataset have arisen by chance. In the language of the statisticians, this means that you need a two tailed test unless you have very convincing evidence that the difference can be in only one direction.

*Were "outliers" analysed with both common sense and appropriate statistical adjustments?*

Unexpected results may reflect idiosyncrasies in the subject (for example, unusual metabolism), errors in measurement (for example, faulty equipment), errors in interpretation (for example, misreading a meter reading), or errors in calculation (for example, misplaced decimal points). Only the first of these is a "real" result that deserves to be included in the analysis. A result that is many orders of magnitude away from the others is less likely to be genuine, but it may be. A few years ago, while doing a research project, I measured a number of different hormone concentrations in about 30 subjects. One subject's growth hormone concentration came back about a hundred times higher than everyone else's. I assumed this was a transcription error so I moved the decimal point two places to the left. Some weeks later I met the technician who had analysed the specimens and he asked "Whatever happened to that chap with acromegaly?"

Statistically correcting for outliers (for example, to modify their effect on the overall result) is quite a sophisticated statistical manoeuvre. If you are interested, try the relevant section in Douglas Altman's book[13].

## 5.4 Correlation, regression, and causation

*Has correlation been distinguished from regression and has the correlation coefficient ("r value") been calculated and interpreted correctly?*

For many non-statisticians, the terms "correlation" and "regression" are synonymous and refer vaguely to a mental image of a scatter graph with dots sprinkled messily along a diagonal line sprouting from the intercept of the axes. You would be right in assuming that if two things are not correlated, it will be meaningless to attempt a regression. But regression and correlation are both precise statistical terms that serve quite different functions[14].

The *r* value (Pearson's product-moment correlation coefficient) is among the most overused statistical instruments in the book. Strictly speaking, the *r* value is not valid unless the following criteria are fulfilled:

- The data (or, strictly, the population from which the data are drawn) should be normally distributed; if they are not, non-parametric tests of correlation should be used instead (see table 5.1)

- The two variables should be structurally independent (that is, one should not be forced to vary with the other)

- Only a single pair of measurements should be made on each subject, since the measurements made on successive subjects need to be statistically independent of each other if we are to end up with unbiased estimates of the population parameters of interest[14]

- Every *r* value should be accompanied by a *p* value, which expresses how likely an association of this strength would be to have arisen by chance, or a confidence interval, which expresses the range within which the "true" *r* value is likely to lie (see section 5.5).

Remember, too, that even if the $r$ value is an appropriate value to calculate from a set of data, it does not tell you whether the relation, however strong, is causal (see below).

What, then, is regression? The term "regression" refers to a mathematical *equation* that allows one variable (the *target* variable) to be predicted from another (the *independent* variable). Regression, then, implies a direction of influence, although as the next section will argue, it does not prove causality. In the case of multiple regression, a far more complex mathematical equation (which, thankfully, usually remains the secret of the computer that calculated it) allows the target variable to be predicted from two or more independent variables (often known as *covariables*).

The simplest regression equation, which you may remember from your schooldays, is $y = a + bx$, where $y$ is the dependent variable (plotted on the vertical axis), $x$ is the independent variable (plotted on the horizontal axis), and $a$ is the $y$ intercept. Not many biological variables can be predicted with such a simple equation. The weight of a group of people, for example, varies with their height, but not in a linear way. I am twice as tall as my son and three times his weight, but although I am four times as tall as my newborn nephew I am much more than six times his weight. Weight, in fact, probably varies more closely with the square of someone's height than with height itself (so that a quadratic rather than a linear regression would probably be more appropriate).

Of course, even when you have fed sufficient height-weight data into a computer for it to calculate the regression equation that best predicts a person's weight from their height, your predictions would still be pretty poor as weight and height are not all that closely *correlated*. There are other things that influence weight in addition to height, and we could, to illustrate the principle of multiple regression, enter data on age, sex, daily calorie intake, and physical activity into the computer and ask it how much each of these convariables contributes to the overall equation (or model).

The elementary principles described here, particularly the points on the previous pages, should help you to spot whether correlation and regression are being used correctly in the paper you are reading. A more detailed discussion on the subject can be found in Martin Bland's textbook[14] and in the fourth article in the "Basic Statistics for Clinicians" series[4].

*Have assumptions been made about the nature and direction of causality?*

Remember the ecological fallacy: just because a town has a large number of unemployed people and a very high crime rate it does not necessarily follow that the unemployed are committing the crimes! In other words, the presence of an *association* between A and B tells you nothing at all about either the presence or the direction of causality. To demonstrate that A has *caused* B (rather than B causing A, or A and B both being caused by C) you need more than a correlation coefficient. Box 5.2 gives some criteria, originally developed by Sir Austin Bradford Hill, that should be met before causality is assumed[15].

---

**Box 5.2 Tests for causation**

- Is there evidence from true experiments in humans?
- Is the association strong?
- Is the association consistent from study to study?
- Is the temporal relation appropriate (that is, did the postulated cause precede the postulated effect)?
- Is there a dose-response gradient (that is, does more of the postulated effect follow more of the postulated cause)?
- Does the association make epidemiological sense?
- Does the association make biological sense?
- Is the association specific?
- Is the association analogous to a previously proved causal association?

Adapted from Haines A. Multipractice research: a cohort study. In: Jones R, Kinmonth AL, eds. *Critical Reading for Primary Care.* Oxford: Oxford University Press, 1995: 124.

---

## 5.5 Probability and confidence

*Have "P values" been calculated and interpreted appropriately?*

One of the first values a student of statistics learns to calculate is the P value—that is, the probability that any particular outcome would have arisen by chance. Standard scientific practice, which is entirely arbitrary, usually deems a P value of less than one in 20 (expressed as $P < 0.05$, and equivalent to a betting odds of 19 to one) as "statistically significant" and a P value of less than one in 100 ($P < 0.01$) as "statistically highly significant".

By definition, then, one chance association in 20 (this must be around one major published result per journal issue) will seem to be significant when it isn't and one in a 100 will seem highly significant when it is really a "fluke". Hence, if you *must* analyse multiple outcomes from your data set you need to make a correction to try to allow for this (usually achieved by the Bonferoni method[16] [17]).

A result in the statistically significant range (P <0.05 or P <0.01 depending on what you have chosen as the cut off) suggests that the authors should reject the null hypothesis (that is, the hypothesis that there is no real difference between two groups). But as I have argued earlier (see above and section 4.6), a P value in the non-significant range tells you that *either* there is no difference between the groups *or* there were too few subjects to demonstrate such a difference if it existed. It does not tell you which.

The P value has a further limitation. Gordon Guyatt and colleagues, in the first article of their "Basic statistics for clinicians" series on hypothesis testing with P values, conclude:

> "Why use a single cut-off point [for statistical significance] when the choice of such a point is arbitrary? Why make the question of whether a treatment is effective a dichotomy (a yes-no decision) when it would be more appropriate to view it as a continuum?"[1]

For this, we need confidence intervals, which are considered next.

*Have confidence intervals been calculated and do the authors' conclusions reflect them?*

A confidence interval, which a good statistician can calculate on the result of just about any statistical test (the *t* test, the *r* value, the absolute risk reduction, the number needed to treat, and the sensitivity, specificity, and other key features of a diagnostic test), allows you to estimate for both "positive" trials (those that show a statistically significant difference between two arms of the trial) and "negative" ones (those that seem to show no difference), whether the strength of the evidence is *strong* or *weak* and whether the study is *definitive* (that is, obviates the need for further similar studies). The calculation of confidence intervals has been covered with great clarity in Martin Gardner and Douglas Altman's book *Statistics with Confidence*[18], and their interpretation has been covered by Guyatt and colleagues[2].

If you repeated the same clinical trial hundreds of times, you would not get exactly the same result each time. But, *on average* you would establish a particular level of difference (or lack of difference!) between the two arms of the trial. In 90% of the trials the difference between two arms would lie within certain broad limits, and in 95% of the trials it would lie between certain, even broader, limits.

Now, if, as is usually the case, you conducted only one trial, how do you know how close the result is to the "real" difference between the groups? The answer is you don't. But by calculating, say, the 95% confidence interval around your result, you will be able to say that there is a 95% chance that the "real" difference lies between these two limits. The sentence to look for in a paper should read something like:

> "In a trial of the treatment of heart failure, 33% of the patients randomised to ACE inhibitors died, whereas 38% of those randomised to hydralazine and nitrates died. The point estimate of the difference between the groups [the best single estimate of the benefit in lives saved from the use of an ACE inhibitor] is 5%. The 95% confidence interval around this difference is -1.2% to +12%".

More likely, the results would be expressed in the following shorthand:

> "The ACE inhibitor group had a 5% (95% confidence interval -1.2 to 12) higher survival".

In this particular example, the 95% confidence interval overlaps zero difference and, if we were expressing the result as a dichotomy (that is, is the hypothesis "proved" or "disproved"?) we would classify it as a negative trial. Yet as Guyatt and colleagues argue, there *probably* is a real difference and it *probably* lies closer to 5% than either -1.2% or 12%. A more useful conclusion from these results is that "all else being equal, ACE inhibitor is the appropriate choice for patients with heart failure, but that the strength of that inference is weak"[2].

As section 8.3 argues, the larger the trial (or the larger the pooled results of several trials), the narrower the confidence interval, and, therefore, the more likely the result is to be definitive.

In interpreting "negative" trials, one important thing you need to know is "would a much larger trial be likely to show a significant benefit?" To answer this question, look at the *upper* 95% confidence limit of the result. There is only once chance in 40 (that is, a 2½%

chance, as the other 2¹/2% of extreme results will lie below the *lower* 95% confidence limit) that the real result will be this much or more. Now ask yourself: "Would this level of difference be *clinically* significant?", and if it wouldn't you can classify the trial as not only negative but also definitive. If, on the other hand, the upper 95% confidence limit represented a clinically significant level of difference between the groups, the trial may be negative but it is also non-definitive.

The use of confidence intervals is still relatively uncommon in medical papers. In one survey of a hundred articles from three top journals (*New England Journal of Medicine, Annals of Internal Medicine,* and *Canadian Medical Association Journal*), only 43% reported any confidence intervals at all, whereas 66% gave a P value[1]. An even smaller proportion of articles interpret their confidence intervals correctly. You should check carefully in the discussion section to see whether the authors have correctly concluded *(a)* whether and to what extent their trial supported their hypothesis and *(b)* whether any further studies need to be done.

## 5.6 The bottom line (quantifying the risk of benefit and harm)

*Have the authors expressed the effects of an intervention in terms of the likely benefit or harm that an individual patient can expect?*

It is all very well to say that a particular intervention produces a "statistically significant difference" in outcome but if I were being asked to take a new medicine I would want to know how much better my chances would be (in terms of any particular outcome) than they would be if I didn't take it. Four simple calculations (and I promise you they *are* simple—if you can add, subtract, multiply, and divide you will be able to follow this section) will enable you to answer this question objectively and in a way that means something to the non-statistician. The calculations are the relative risk reduction, the absolute risk reduction, the number needed to treat, and the odds ratio.

To illustrate these concepts, and to persuade you that you need to know about them, let me tell you about a survey that Tom Fahey and his colleagues conducted recently[19]. They wrote to 182 board members of district health authorities in England (all of whom would be in some way responsible for making important health service decisions) and put the following data to them about four different rehabilitation programmes for heart attack victims. They asked which one they would prefer to fund:

● Programme A—which reduced the rate of deaths by 20%

● Programme B—which produced an absolute reduction in deaths of 3%

● Programme C—which increased patients' survival rate from 84% to 87%

● Programme D—which meant that 31 people needed to enter the programme to avoid one death.

Of the 140 board members who responded, only three spotted that all four "programmes" in fact related to the same set of results. The other 137 all selected one of the programmes in preference to one of the others, thus revealing (as well as their own ignorance) the need for better basic training in epidemiology for health authority board members.

Table 5.2 Effect of coronary artery bypass graft on survival

| Treatment | Outcome at 10 years | | Total number of patients randomised in each group |
|---|---|---|---|
| | Dead | Alive | |
| Medical | 404 | 921 | 1324 |
| Surgery | 350 | 974 | 1325 |

Let's use the example in table 5.2, which Fahey and colleagues reproduced from a study by Salim Yusuf and colleagues[20]. I have expressed the figures as a two by two table giving details of which treatment the patients received in their randomised trial and whether they were dead or alive 10 years later.

Simple maths tells you that patients on medical treatment have a 404/1324 = 0.305 or 30.5% chance of being dead at 10 years. Let's call this risk $x$. Patients randomised to coronary artery bypass graft have a 350/1325 = 0.264 or 26.4% chance of being dead at 10 years. Let's call this risk $y$.

The relative risk of death—that is, the risk in surgery patients compared with controls—is $y/x$ or 0.264/0.305 = 0.87 (87%).

The relative risk reduction—that is, the amount by which the risk of death is reduced by surgery—is 100% - 87% $(1 - y/x) = 13\%$.

The absolute risk reduction (or risk difference)—that is, the absolute amount by which surgery reduces the risk of death at 10 years—is 30.5% - 26.4% = 4.1% (0.041).

The number needed to treat—that is, how many patients need a bypass graft to prevent, on average, one death by 10 years—is the reciprocal of the absolute risk reduction, 1/ARR = 1/0.041 = 24.

The final way of expressing the effect of treatment that I want to introduce here is the odds ratio. Look back at table 5.2 and you will see that the "odds" of dying compared with the "odds" of surviving for patients in the medical treatment group are 404/921 = 0.44 and for patients in the surgery group are 350/974 = 0.36. The *ratio* of these odds will be 0.36/0.44 = 0.82.

The general formulas for calculating these "bottom line" effects of an intervention are reproduced in appendix D, and for a discussion on which of these values is most useful in which circumstances see Jaenschke and colleagues' article in the "Basic Statistics for Clinicians" series[3] or chapter 7 (Deciding on the best therapy) of Sackett *et al's* clinical epidemiology textbook[21].

## 5.7 Summary

It is possible to be seriously misled by taking the statistical competence (or the intellectual honesty) of authors for granted. Statistics can be an intimidating science, and understanding its finer points often calls for expert help. But I hope that this chapter has shown you that the statistics used in most medical research papers can be evaluated by the non-expert using a simple checklist such as that in appendix A. In addition, you might like to check the paper you are reading (or writing) against the common errors given in box 5.1.

[1] Guyatt G, Jaenschke R, Heddle N, *et al*. Basic statistics for clinicians. 1. Hypothesis testing. *Can Med Assoc J* 1995: **152**: 27-32.

[2] Guyatt G, Jaenschke R, Heddle N, *et al*. Basic statistics for clinicians. 2. Interpreting study results: confidence intervals. *Can Med Assoc J* 1995: **152**: 169-73.

[3] Jaenschke R, Guyatt G, Shannon H, *et al*. Basic statistics for clinicians. 3. Assessing the effects of treatment: measures of association. *Can Med Assoc J* 1995: **152**: 351-7.

4  Guyatt G, Walter S, Shannon H, *et al.* Basic statistics for clinicians. 4. Correlation and regression. *Can Med Assoc J* 1995: **152**: 497-504.

5  Bland M. *An introduction to medical statistics.* Oxford: Oxford University Press, 1987.

6  Altman D. *Practical statistics for medical research.* London: Chapman & Hall, 1995; 461-2.

7  Bland M. *An introduction to medical statistics.* Oxford: Oxford University Press, 1987, 112-29.

8  Hughes MD, Pocock SJ. Stopping rules and estimation problems in clinical trials. *Stat Med* 1987; 7: 1231-42.

9  Stewart LA, Parmar MKB. Bias in the analysis and reporting of randomized controlled trials. *Int J Health Technol Assess* 1996; **12**: 264-75.

10 Canadian Cooperative Stroke Group. A randomised trial of aspirin and sulfinpyrazone in threatened stroke. *N Engl J Med* 1978; **299**: 53-9.

11 Antiplatelet Trialists Collaboration. Secondary prevention of vascular disease by prolonged antiplatelet treatment. *BMJ* 1988; **296**: 320-1.

12 Oxman AD, Guyatt GH. A consumer's guide to subgroup analysis. *Ann Intern Med* 1992; **116**: 79-84.

13 Altman D. *Practical statistics for medical research.* London: Chapman & Hall, 1985; 126-30.

14 Bland M. *An introduction to medical statistics.* Oxford: Oxford University Press, 1987; 188-215.

15 Bradford Hill, A. The environment and disease: association or causation? *Proc R Soc Med.* 1965; **58**: 295-300. (Adapted version is reproduced with permission from Haines A. Multi-practice research: a cohort study. In: Jones R, Kinmouth A-L, eds. *Critical reading for primary care.* Oxford: Oxford University Press, 1995: p124.)

16 Altman D. *Practical statistics for medical research.* London: Chapman & Hall, 1995; 210-2.

17 Pocock SJ, Geller XPL, Tsiatis AA. The analysis of multiple endpoints in clinical trials. *Biometrics.* 1987; **43**: 487-98.

18 Gardner MJ, Altman DG, eds. *Statistics with confidence: confidence intervals and statistical guidelines.* London: BMJ Publishing, 1989.

19 Fahey T, Griffiths S, Peters TJ. Evidence-based purchasing: understanding the results of clinical trials and systematic reviews. *BMJ* 1995, 311: 1056–60.

20 Yusuf S, Zucker D, Peduzzi P, *et al.* Effect of coronary artery bypass surgery on survival: overview of ten year results from randomized trials by the coronary artery surgery trialists collaboration. *Lancet* 1994; **344**: 563-70.

21 Sackett DL, Haynes RB, Guyatt GH, *et al. Clinical epidemiology - a basic science for clinical medicine.* London: Little, Brown, 1991; 187-248.

# Chapter 6: Papers that report drug trials

## 6.1 "Evidence" and marketing

If you are a clinical doctor or nurse practitioner (that is, if you prescribe drugs) the pharmaceutical industry is interested in you and spends a proportion of its multimillion pound annual advertising budget trying to influence you (see box 6.1). The most effective way of changing the prescribing habits of a clinician is through a personal representative (known to most of us in the UK as the "drug rep" and to our North American colleagues as the "detailer"), who travels round with a briefcase full of "evidence" in support of his or her wares[1].

As sections 3.4 and 3.6 argued, questions about the benefits of treatment should ideally be examined with randomised controlled trials. But preliminary questions about pharmacokinetics (that is, how the drug behaves while it is getting to its site of action), particularly those relating to bioavailability, require a straight dosing experiment in healthy (and, if ethical and practicable, sick) volunteers.

Common (and hopefully trivial) adverse drug reactions may be picked up and their incidence quantified in the randomised controlled trials undertaken to demonstrate the drug's efficacy. But rare (and usually more serious) adverse drug reactions require both pharmacovigilance surveys (collection of data prospectively on patients receiving a newly licensed drug) and case-control studies (see section 3.4) to establish association[2]. Ideally, individual rechallenge experiments (where the patient who has had

---

## Box 6.1 Ten tips for the pharmaceutical industry: how to present your product in the best light

- Think up a plausible physiological mechanism why the drug works and become slick at presenting it. Preferably, find a surrogate end point that is heavily influenced by the drug, though it may not be strictly valid (see section 6.2)
- When designing clinical trials, select a patient population, clinical features, and trial length that reflect the maximum possible response to the drug
- If possible, compare your product only with placebos. If you must compare it with a competitor, make sure the latter is given at subtherapeutic dose
- Include the results of pilot studies in the figures for definitive studies ("Russian doll publication"), so it looks like more patients have been randomised than is actually the case
- Omit mention of any trial that had a fatality or serious adverse drug reaction in the treatment group. If possible, don't publish such studies
- Get your graphics department to maximise the visual impact of your message. It helps not to label the axes of graphs or say whether scales are linear or logarithmic. Make sure you do not show individual patient data or confidence intervals
- Become master of the hanging comparative ("better" but better than what?)
- Invert the standard hierarchy of evidence so that anecdote takes precedence over randomised trials and meta-analyses
- Name at least three local opinion leaders who use the drug and offer "starter packs" for the doctor to try
- Present a "cost-effectiveness" analysis that shows that your product, even though more expensive than its competitor, "actually works out cheaper" (see section 10.1)

---

a reaction considered to be caused by the drug is given the drug again in carefully supervised circumstances) should be performed to establish causation[3].

Pharmaceutical "reps" do not tell nearly as many lies as they used to (drug marketing has become an altogether more sophisticated science), but they have been known to cultivate a shocking ignorance of basic epidemiology and clinical trial design when it suits them[4]. It often helps their case, for example, to present the results of uncontrolled trials and express them in terms of before and after differences in a particular outcome measure.[5] Reference back to section 3.6 and a look at the recent *Lancet* series of placebo effects[6-12] should remind you why uncontrolled before and after studies are the stuff of teenage magazines, not hard science.

Dr Andrew Herxheimer, who edited *Drug and Therapeutics Bulletin* for many years, is currently undertaking a survey of "references" cited in advertisements for pharmaceutical products in the leading UK medical journals. He tells me that a high proportion of such references cite "data on file", and many more refer to publications written, edited, and published entirely by the industry. Evidence from these sources has sometimes (though by no means invariably) been shown to be of lower scientific quality than that which appears in independent, peer reviewed journals[4]. And let's face it, if you worked for a drug company that had made a major scientific breakthrough you would probably submit your findings to a publication such as the *Lancet* or the *New England Journal of Medicine* in addition to publishing them in house. In other words, you don't need to "trash" papers about drug trials *because* of where they have been published, but you do need to look closely at the methodology and statistical analysis of such trials.

## 6.2 Making decisions about treatment

Sackett and colleagues, in their book *Clinical epidemiology a basic science for clinical medicine*[13], argue that before starting a patient on a drug, the doctor should:

- Identify *for this patient* the ultimate objective of treatment (cure, prevention of recurrence, limitation of functional disability, prevention of later complications, reassurance, palliation, symptomatic relief, etc)

- Select the *most appropriate* treatment by using all available evidence (this includes examining the question of whether the patient needs to take any drug at all)

- Specify the *treatment target* (how will you know when to stop treatment, change its intensity, or switch to some other treatment?)

For example, in the treatment of high blood pressure, the doctor might decide that:

- The *ultimate objective of treatment* is to prevent [further] target organ damage to brain, eye, heart, kidney, etc (and thereby prevent death)

- The *choice of specific treatment* is between the various classes of antihypertensive drug selected on the basis of randomised, placebo controlled, and comparative trials, as well as between non-drug treatments such as salt restriction

- The *treatment target* might be a phase V diastolic blood pressure (right arm, sitting) of less than 90 mm Hg or as close to that as tolerable in the face of drug side effects.

If these three steps are not followed (as is often the case—for example, in terminal care) therapeutic chaos can result. In a veiled slight on surrogate end points, Sackett and his team remind us that the choice of specific treatment should be determined by evidence of what *does* work and not on what *seems* to work or *ought* to work. "Today's therapy", they warn (page 188), "when derived from biologic facts or uncontrolled clinical experience, may become tomorrow's bad joke"[13].

## 6.3  Surrogate end points

I have not included this section solely because it is a particular hobby horse of mine. If you are a practising (and non-academic) clinician, your main contact with published papers may well be through what gets fed to you by a "drug rep". The pharmaceutical industry is a slick player at the surrogate end point game, and I make no apology for labouring the point that such outcome measures must be evaluated very carefully.

I will define a surrogate end point as *"a variable that is relatively easily measured and that predicts a rare or distant outcome of either a toxic stimulus (for example, pollutant) or a therapeutic intervention (for example, surgical procedure, piece of advice), but which is not itself a direct measure of either harm or clinical benefit"*. The growing interest in surrogate end points in medical research reflects two important features of their use:

- They can considerably reduce the *sample size, duration,* and, therefore, *cost,* of clinical trials

- They can allow treatments to be assessed in situations when the use of primary outcomes would be excessively *invasive* or *unethical.*

In the evaluation of pharmaceutical products, commonly used surrogate end points include:

- Pharmacokinetic measurements (for example, concentration-time curves of a drug or its active metabolite in the bloodstream)

- In vitro (that is, laboratory) measures such as the mean inhibitory concentration (MIC) of an antimicrobial against a bacterial culture on agar

- Macroscopic appearance of tissues (for example, gastric erosion seen at endoscopy)

- Change in concentrations of [alleged] "serum markers of disease" (for example, prostate specific antigen[14])

- Radiological appearance (for example, shadowing on a chest *x* ray).

Surrogate end points have several drawbacks. Firstly, a change in the surrogate end point does not itself answer the essential preliminary questions: "What is the objective of treatment in this patient?" and "What, according to valid and reliable research studies, is the best available treatment for this condition?" Secondly, the surrogate end point may not closely reflect the treatment target—in other words, it may not be valid or reliable. Thirdly, the use of a surrogate end point has the same limitations as the use of any other *single* measure of the success or failure of treatment—it ignores all the other measures! Over-reliance on a single surrogate end point as a measure of therapeutic success usually reflects a narrow or naïve clinical perspective.

Finally, surrogate end points are often developed in animal models of disease so that changes in a specific variable can be measured under controlled conditions in a well defined population. Extrapolation of these findings to human disease, however, is liable to be invalid[15-17].

- In animal studies, the population being studied has fairly uniform biological characteristics and may be genetically inbred

- Both the tissue and the disease being studied may vary in important characteristics (for example, susceptibility to the pathogen, rate of cell replication) from the parallel condition in human subjects

- The animals are kept in a controlled environment that minimises the influence of lifestyle variables (for example, diet, exercise, stress) and concomitant medication

- Giving high doses of chemicals to experimental animals may distort the usual metabolic pathways and thereby give misleading results. Animal species best suited to serve as a surrogate for humans vary for different chemicals.

The ideal features of a surrogate end point are shown in box 6.2. If the "rep" who is trying to persuade you of the value of the drug cannot justify the end points used, you should challenge him or her to produce additional evidence.

One important example of the invalid use of a surrogate end point is the CD4 cell count (a measure of one type of white blood cell which, when I was at medical school, was known as the "T helper cell") in monitoring progression to AIDS in HIV positive subjects. The CONCORDE trial was a randomised controlled trial comparing early versus late initiation of zidovudine treatment in patients who were HIV positive but clinically asymptomatic[18]. Previous studies had shown that early initiation of treatment led to a slower decline in the CD4 cell count (a variable that had been shown to fall with the progression of AIDS), and it was assumed that a higher CD4 cell count would reflect improved chances of survival.

The CONCORDE trial, however, showed that while CD4 cell counts fell more slowly in the treatment group, the survival rates at three years were identical in the two groups. This experience confirmed a warning issued earlier by authors suspicious of the validity of this end point[19]. Subsequent research has attempted to identify a surrogate end point that correlates with real therapeutic benefit—that is, progression of asymptomatic HIV infection to clinical AIDS and survival time after the onset of AIDS[20][21]. Using multiple regression analysis, investigators in the United States found that a combination of several markers (proportion of CD4 C29 cells, degree of fatigue, age, and haemoglobin concentration) was the best predictor of progression[20].

## Box 6.2  Ideal features of a surrogate end point

- The surrogate end point should be reliable, reproducible, clinically available, easily quantifiable, affordable, and exhibit a "dose-response" effect (that is, the higher the level of the surrogate end point, the greater the probability of disease)
- It should be a true predictor of disease (or risk of disease) and not merely express exposure to a covariable. The relation between the surrogate end point and the disease should have a biologically plausible explanation
- It should be sensitive—that is, a "positive" result for the surrogate end point should pick up all or most patients at increased risk of adverse outcome
- It should be specific—that is, a "negative" result should exclude all or most of those without increased risk of adverse outcome
- There should be a precise cut off between normal and abnormal values
- It should have an acceptable positive predictive value—that is, a "positive" result should always or usually mean that the patient thus identified is at increased risk of adverse outcome (see section 7.2)
- It should have an acceptable negative predictive value—that is, a "negative" result should always or usually mean that the patient thus identified is not at increased risk of adverse outcome (see section 7.2)
- It should be amenable to quality control monitoring
- Changes in the surrogate end point should rapidly and accurately reflect the response to treatment—in particular, levels should normalise in states of remission or cure

If you think this is an isolated example of the world's best scientists all barking up the wrong tree in pursuit of a bogus end point, check out the literature on the use of ventricular premature beats (a minor irregularity of the heartbeat) to predict death from serious heart rhythm disturbance[22] [23], blood concentrations of antibiotics to predict clinical cure of infection[24], or plaques on magnetic resonance imaging to chart the progression of multiple sclerosis[25]. You might also like to see the fascinating literature on the development of valid and relevant surrogate end points in the important field of cancer prevention[26].

Clinicians are increasingly sceptical of arguments for using new drugs, or old drugs in new indications, that are not justified by direct evidence of effectiveness. Before surrogate end points can be used in the marketing of pharmaceuticals those in the industry must justify the utility of these measures by demonstrating a plausible and consistent link between the end point and the development or progression of disease.

It would be wrong to suggest that the pharmaceutical industry develops surrogate end points with the deliberate intention to mislead the licensing authorities and health professionals. Surrogate end points have both ethical and economic imperatives. The industry does, however, have a vested interest in overstating its case on the strength of these end points. Given that much of the data relating to the validation of surrogate end points are not currently presented in published clinical papers and that the development of such markers is often a lengthy and expensive process, one author has suggested the setting up of a data archive that would pool data across studies[27].

## 6.4 How to get evidence out of a "drug rep"

Any doctor who has ever given an audience to a "rep" who is selling a non-steroidal anti-inflammatory drug will recognise the gastric erosion example. The question to ask him or her is not "What is the incidence of gastric erosion on your drug?" but "What is the incidence of potentially life threatening gastric bleeding?" Other questions to ask "drug reps", reproduced from an article in *Drug and Therapeutics Bulletin*[28] and other sources[13][15], are listed below:

- See representatives only by appointment. Choose to see only those whose product interests you and confine the interview to that product

- Take charge of the interview. Do not hear out a rehearsed sales routine but ask directly for the information below

- Request independent published evidence from reputable peer reviewed journals

- Do not look at promotional brochures, which often contain unpublished material, misleading graphs, and selective quotations

- Ignore anecdotal "evidence" such as the fact that a medical celebrity is prescribing the product

- Using the "STEP" acronym, ask for evidence in four specific areas:

  - Safety—that is, likelihood of long term or serious side effects caused by the drug (remember that rare but serious adverse reactions to new drugs may be poorly documented)[2]

  - Tolerability, which is best measured by comparing the pooled withdrawal rates between the drug and its most significant competitor

  - Efficacy, of which the most relevant dimension is how the product compares with your current favourite

  - Price, which should take into account indirect as well as direct costs (see section 10.3).

- Evaluate the evidence stringently, paying particular attention to the power (sample size) and methodological quality of clinical trials and the use of surrogate end points. Do not accept theoretical arguments in the drug's favour (for example, "longer half life") without direct evidence that this translates into clinical benefit

- Do not accept the newness of a product as an argument for changing to it. Indeed, there are good scientific arguments for doing the opposite[29]

- Decline to try the product through starter packs or by participating in small scale uncontrolled "research" studies

- Record in writing the content of the interview and return to these notes if the rep requests another audience.

1 Shaughnessy AF, Slawson DC. Pharmaceutical representatives. *BMJ* 1996: **312**: 1494-5.
2 Buckley NA, Smith AJ. Evidence-based medicine in toxicology: where is the evidence? *Lancet* 1996; **347**: 1167–9.
3 Sackett DL, Haynes RB, Guyatt GH, *et al. Clinical epidemiology - a basic science for clinical medicine.* London: Little, Brown, 1991; 297-301.
4 Bardelay D. Visits from medical representatives: fine principles, poor practice. *Prescrire International* 1995; **4**: 120-2.

5 Bero LA, Rennie D. Influences on the quality of published drug studies. *Int J Health Technol Assess* 1996; **12**: 209-37.

6 Kleijnen J, de Craen AJ, van Everdingen J, *et al*. Placebo effect in double-blind clinical trials: a review of interactions with medications. *Lancet* 1994; **344**: 1347-9.

7 Joyce CR. Placebo and complementary medicine. *Lancet* 1994; **344**: 1279-81.

8 Laporte JR, Figueras A. Placebo effects in psychiatry. *Lancet* 1994; **344**: 1206-9.

9 Johnson AG. Surgery as a placebo. *Lancet* 1994; **344**: 1140-2.

10 Thomas KB. The placebo in general practice. *Lancet* 1994; **344**: 1066-7.

11 Chaput de Saintonge DM, Herxheimer A. Harnessing placebo effects in health care. *Lancet* 1994; **344**: 995-8.

12 Gotzsche PC. Is there logic in the placebo? *Lancet* 1994; **344**: 925-6.

13 Sackett DL, Haynes RB, Guyatt GH, *et al*. *Clinical epidemiology - a basic science for clinical medicine*. London: Little, Brown, 1991; 187-248.

14 Bostwick DG, Burke HB, Wheeler TM, *et al*. The most promising surrogate endpoint biomarkers for screening candidate chemopreventive compounds for prostatic adenocarcinoma in short-term Phase II clinical trials. *J Cell Biochem* 1994; suppl 19; 283-9.

15 Gøtzsche P, Liberati A, Torri V, *et al*. Beware of surrogate outcome measures. *Int J Health Technol Assess* 1996; **12**: 238-46.

16 Lipkin M. Summary of recommendations for colonic biomarker studies of candidate chemopreventive compounds in phase II clinical trials. *J Cell Biochem* 1994; suppl 19: 94-8.

17 Kimbrough RD. Determining acceptable risks: experimental and epidemiological issues. *Clin Chem* 1994; **40**: 1448-53.

18 CONCORDE Coordinating Committee. CONCORDE MRC/ANRS randomised double-blind controlled trial of immediate and deferred zidovudine in symptom-free HIV infection. *Lancet* 1994; **343**: 871-81.

19 Jacobson MA, Bacchetti P, Kolokathis A, *et al*. Surrogate markers for survival in patients with AIDS and AIDS related complex treated with zidovudine. *BMJ* 1991; **302**: 73-8.

20 Blatt SP, McCarthy WF, Bucko-Krasnicka B, *et al*. Multivariate models for predicting progression to AIDS and survival in HIV-infected patients. *J Infect Dis* 1995; **171**: 837-44.

21 Tsoukas CM, Bernard NF. Markers predicting progression of HIV-related disease. *Clin Microbiol Rev* 1994; **7**: 14-28.

22 Epstein AE, Hallstrom AO, Rogers WJ, *et al*. Mortality following ventricular arrhythmia suppression by encainide, flecainide and moricizine after myocardial infarction. *JAMA* 1993; **270**: 2451-5.

23 Lipicky RJ, Packer M. Role of surrogate endpoints in the evaluation of drugs for heart failure. *J Am Coll Cardiol* 1993; **22** (suppl A); 179-84.

24 Hyatt JM, McKinnon PS, Zimmer GS, *et al*. The importance of pharmacokinetic/pharmacodynamic surrogate markers to outcome. Focus on antibacterial agents. *Clin Pharmacokinetics* 1995; **28**: 143-60.

25 Anonymous. Interferon beta-1b—hope or hype? *Drug Ther Bull* 1996; **34**: 9-11.

26 Entire issue of *J Cell Biochem* 1994; suppl 19.

27 Aicken M. If there is gold in the labelling index hills, are we digging in the right place? *J Cell Biochem* 1994; suppl 19; 91-3.

28 Anonymous. Getting good value from drug reps. *Drug Ther Bull* 1983; **21**: 13-5.

29 Ferner RE. Newly licensed drugs. *BMJ* 1996; **313**: 1157-8.

# Chapter 7: Papers that report diagnostic or screening tests

## 7.1 Ten men in the dock

If you are new to the concept of validating diagnostic tests and if algebraic explanations ("let's call this value *x*...") leave you cold, the following example may help you. Ten men are awaiting trial for murder. Only three of them actually committed a murder; the other seven are innocent of any crime. A jury hears each case, and finds six of the men guilty of murder. Two of the convicted are true murderers. Four men are wrongly imprisoned. One murderer walks free.

This information can be expressed in what is known as a two by two table (table 7.1). Note that the "truth" (that is, whether or not the men really committed a murder) is expressed along the horizontal title row, whereas the jury's verdict (which may or may not reflect the truth) is expressed down the vertical title row.

You should be able to see that these figures, if they are typical, reflect several features of this particular jury:

Table 7.1   2x2 Table showing outcome of trial for ten men accused of murder

| Jury verdict | True criminal status | |
|---|---|---|
| | Murderer | Not murderer |
| "Guilty" | Rightly convicted: **2** men | Wrongly convicted: **4** men |
| "Innocent" | Wrongly acquitted: **1** man | Rightly acquitted: **3** men |

- The jury correctly identifies two in every three true murderers

- It correctly acquits three out of every seven innocent people

- If this jury has found a person guilty, there is still only a one in three chance that they are actually a murderer

- If this jury found a person innocent, he has a three in four chance of actually being innocent

- In five cases out of every ten the jury gets the verdict right.

These five features constitute, respectively, the sensitivity, specificity, positive predictive value, negative predictive value, and accuracy of this jury's performance. The rest of this chapter considers these five features applied to diagnostic (or screening) tests when compared with a "true" diagnosis or gold standard. Section 7.4 also introduces a sixth, slightly more complicated (but very useful), feature of a diagnostic test—the likelihood ratio. (After you have read the rest of this chapter, look back at this section. You should, by then, be able to work out that the likelihood ratio of a positive jury verdict in the above example is 1.17 and that of a negative one 0.78. If you can't, don't worry—many eminent clinicians have no idea what a likelihood ratio is.)

## 7.2 Validating diagnostic tests against a gold standard

Our window cleaner told me the other day that he had been feeling thirsty recently and had asked his general practitioner to be tested for diabetes, which runs in his family. The nurse in his general practitioner's surgery had asked him to produce a urine specimen and dipped a special stick in it. The stick stayed blue, which meant, apparently, that there was no sugar (glucose) in his urine. This, the nurse had said, meant that he did not have diabetes.

I had trouble explaining to the window cleaner that the test result did not necessarily mean this at all, any more than a guilty verdict *necessarily* makes someone a murderer. The definition of diabetes, according to the World Health Organisation, is a blood glucose concentration above 8 mmol/L in the fasting state or above 11 mmol/L two hours after a 100 g oral glucose load (the much dreaded "glucose tolerance test", in which the subject has to glug down every last drop of a sickly glucose drink and wait two hours for a blood test). These values must be achieved on two separate occasions if the person has no symptoms but on only one occasion if they have typical symptoms of diabetes (thirst, passing large amounts of urine, and so on)[1].

These stringent criteria can be termed the *gold standard* for diagnosing diabetes. In other words, if you fulfil the WHO criteria you can call yourself diabetic, and if you don't, you can't (although some critics have, in fact, challenged this notion[2].) The same cannot be said for dipping a stick into a random urine specimen. For one thing, you might be a true diabetic but have a high renal threshold—that is, your kidneys conserve glucose much better than most people's so your blood glucose concentration would have to be much higher than most people's for any glucose to appear in your urine. Alternatively, you may be an otherwise normal individual with a *low* renal threshold, so glucose leaks into your urine even when there isn't any excess in your blood. In fact, as anyone with diabetes will tell you, diabetes is very often associated with a negative test result for urine glucose.

There are, however, many advantages in using a urine dipstick rather than the full blown glucose tolerance test to "screen" people for diabetes. The test is cheap, convenient, easy to perform and interpret, acceptable to patients, and gives an instant yes or no result. In real life, people like my window cleaner may decline to take an oral glucose tolerance test. Even if he was prepared to go ahead with it, his general practitioner might decide that the window cleaner's symptoms did not merit the expense of this relatively sophisticated investigation. I hope you can see that even though the urine test cannot say for sure if someone is diabetic, it has a definite practical edge over the gold standard. That, of course, is why we use it!

To assess objectively just how useful the urine glucose test for diabetes is, we would need to select a sample of people (say 100) and do two tests on each of them: the urine test (screening test), and a standard glucose tolerance test (gold standard). We could then see, for each person, whether the result of the screening test matched the gold standard. Such an exercise is known as a *validation study*. We could express the results of the validation study in a two by two table (also known as a two by two matrix) as in table 7.2 and calculate various features of the test as in table 7.4 just as we did for the features of the jury in section 7.1.

If the values for the various features of a test (such as sensitivity

Table 7.2  2x2 Table notation  for expressing the results of a validation study for a diagnostic or screening test

| | **Result of gold standard test** | |
|---|---|---|
| **Result of screening test** | Disease positive **a + c** | Disease negative **b + d** |
| Test positive **a + b** | True positive: **a** | False positive: **b** |
| Test negative **c + d** | False negative: **c** | True negative: **d** |

and specificity) fell within reasonable limits, we would be able to say that the test was *valid* (see question 7 below). The validity of testing urine for glucose in the diagnosis of diabetes has been looked at by Andersson and colleagues[3], whose data I have used in the example in table 7.3. The original study was performed on 3268 subjects, of whom 67 either refused to produce a specimen or, for some other reason, were not adequately tested. For simplicity's sake, I have ignored these irregularities and expressed the results in terms of a denominator (total number tested) of 1000 subjects.

Table 7.3  2x2 Table showing results of validation study of urine glucose testing for diabetes against gold standard of glucose tolerance test

| | **Result of glucose tolerance test** | |
|---|---|---|
| **Result of urine test for glucose** | Diabetes positive **27 subjects** | Diabetes negative **973 subjects** |
| Glucose present **13 subjects** | True positive: **6** | False positive: **7** |
| Glucose absent **987 subjects** | False negative: **21** | True negative: **966** |

In actual fact these data came from an epidemiological survey to detect the prevalence of diabetes in a population; the validation of urine testing was a side issue to the main study. If the validation had been the main aim of the study, the subjects selected would have included far more people with diabetes, as question 2 in section 7.3 below will show. If you look up the original paper, you will also find that the gold standard for diagnosing true diabetes was not the oral glucose tolerance test but a more unconventional series of observations. Nevertheless, the example serves its purpose

| Feature of the test | Alternative name | Question that the feature examines | Formula (see tables 7.1, 7.2 and 7.4) |
|---|---|---|---|
| Sensitivity | True positive rate (**P**ositive in **D**isease) | How good is this test at picking up people who have the condition? | a/a+c |
| Specificity | True negative rate (**N**egative in **H**ealth) | How good is this test at correctly excluding people without the condition? | d/b+d |
| Positive predictive value | Post-test probability of a positive test | If a person tests positive, what is the probability that (s)he has the condition? | a/a+b |
| Negative predictive value | Post-test probability of a negative test | If a person tests negative, what is the probability that (s)he does not have the condition? | d/c+d |
| Accuracy | | What proportion of all tests have given the correct result (that is, true positives and true negatives as a proportion of all results | (a+d)/(a+b+c+d) |
| Likelihood ratio of a positive test | | How much more likely is a positive result to be found in a person with, as opposed to without, the condition? | sensitivity/ (1-specificity) |

Table 7.4 Features of a diagnostic test that can be calculated by comparing it with a gold standard in a validation study

as it provides us with some figures to put through the equations listed in the last column of table 7.4. We can calculate the important feature of the urine test for diabetes as follows:

- Sensitivity = a/a+c = 6/27 = 22.2%

- Specificity = d/b+d = 966/973 = 99.3%

- Positive predictive value = a/a+b = 6/13 = 46.2%

- Negative predictive value = d/c+d = 966/987 = 97.8%

- Accuracy = (a+d)/(a+b+c+d) = 972/1000 = 97.2%

- Likelihood ratio of a positive result = sensitivity/(1 - specificity) = 22.2/0.7 = 32

- Likelihood ratio of a negative result = (1 - sensitivity) / specificity = 77.8/99.3 = 0.78.

From these features, you can probably see why I did not share the window cleaner's assurance that he did not have diabetes. A positive urine glucose test is only 22% sensitive, which means that the test misses nearly four fifths of true diabetics. In the presence of classical symptoms and a family history, the window cleaner's baseline chances (pretest likelihood) of having the condition are pretty high, and it is reduced to only about four fifths of this (the negative likelihood ratio, 0.78; see section 7.4) after a single negative urine test. In view of his symptoms, this man clearly needs to undergo a more definitive test for diabetes.

## 7.3 Ten questions to ask about a paper that claims to validate a diagnostic or screening test

In preparing the tips below, I have drawn on three main published sources: the "Users' guides to the medical literature"[4] [5] and the book by the same authors[6]; a more recent article in the *Journal of the American Medical Association*[7], and David Mant's simple and pragmatic guidelines for "testing a test"[8].

*Question 1—Is this test potentially relevant to my practice?*

This is the "so what?" question that Sackett and colleagues call the *utility* of the test[6]. Even if this test were 100% valid, accurate, and reliable, would it help me? Would it identify a treatable disorder? If so, would I use it in preference to the test I use now? Could I (or my patients or the taxpayer) afford it? Would my patients consent to it? Would it change the probabilities for competing diagnoses sufficiently for me to alter my treatment plan? If the answers to these questions are all "no", you may be able to reject the paper (and the test) without reading further than the abstract or introduction.

*Question 2—Has the test been compared with a true gold standard?*

You need to ask, firstly, whether the test has been compared with anything at all! Papers have occasionally been written (and, in the past, published) in which nothing has been done except perform the new test on a few dozen subjects. This exercise may give a range of possible results for the test, but it certainly does not confirm that the "high" results indicate that target disorder (the disease you are looking for) is present or that the "low" results indicate that it isn't.

Next, you should verify that the "gold standard" test used in the survey merits the term. A good way of assessing a gold standard is to use the "so what?" questions listed above. For many conditions, there is no absolute gold standard diagnostic test that will say for certain if it is present or not. Unsurprisingly, these tend to be the very conditions for which new tests are most actively sought. Hence, the authors of such papers may need to develop and justify a combination of criteria against which the new test is to be assessed. One specific point to check is that the test being validated here (or a variant of it) is not being used to contribute to the definition of the gold standard.

*Question 3—Did this validation study include an appropriate spectrum of subjects?*

If you validated a new test for cholesterol in 100 healthy male medical students, you would not be able to say how the test would perform in women, children, older people, those with diseases that seriously raise the cholesterol concentration, or even those who had never been to medical school! Although few people would be naive enough to select quite such a biased sample for the validation study, only 27% of published studies explicity define the spectrum of subjects tested in terms of age, sex, symptoms or severity of disease or both, and specific eligibility criteria[7].

Definition of both the range of participants and the spectrum of disease to be included is essential if the values for the different features of the test are to be worth quoting—that is, if they are to be transferable to other settings. A particular diagnostic test may, conceivably, be more sensitive in women than men or in younger rather than older subjects. For the same reasons, as Sackett and colleagues stipulate, the subjects on which any test is verified should include those with both mild and severe disease, treated and untreated, and those with different but commonly confused conditions[6].

While the sensitivity and specificity of a test are virtually constant whatever the prevalence of the condition, the positive and negative predictive values are crucially dependent on prevalence. This why general practitioners are, often rightly, sceptical of the utility of tests developed exclusively in a secondary care population, where the severity of disease tends to be greater (see section 4.2) and why a good *diagnostic* test (generally used when the patient has some symptoms suggestive of the disease in question) is not necessarily a good *screening* test (generally used in people without symptoms, who are drawn from a population with a much lower prevalence of the disease).

*Question 4—Has work up bias been avoided?*

This is easy to check. It simply means, "Did everyone who got the new diagnostic test also get the gold standard test and vice versa?" I hope you have no problem spotting the potential bias in studies in which the gold standard test is performed only on people who have already tested positive for the test being validated. There are, in addition, a number of more subtle aspects of work up bias that are beyond the scope of this book. If you are interested, you could follow the discussion on this subject in Read and colleagues' paper[7].

*Question 5—Has expectation bias been avoided?*

Expectation bias occurs when pathologists and others who interpret diagnostic specimens are subconsciously influenced by the knowledge of the particular features of the case—for example, the presence of chest pain when they are interpreting an electrocardiogram. In the context of validating diagnostic tests against a gold standard, the question means, "Did the people who interpreted one of the tests know what result the other test had shown on each particular subject?" As I explained in section 4.5, all assessments should be "blind"—that is, the person interpreting the test should not be given any inkling of what the result is expected to be in any particular case.

*Question 6—Was the test shown to be reproducible both within and between observers?*

If the same observer performs the same test on two occasions on a subject whose characteristics have not changed, they will get different results in a proportion of cases. All tests show this feature to some extent, but a test with a reproducibility of 99% is clearly in a different league from one with a reproducibility of 50%. Several factors may contribute to the poor reproducibility of a diagnostic test: the technical precision of the equipment, observer variability (for example, in comparing a colour with a reference chart), arithmetical errors, and so on.

Look back again at page 62 to remind yourself of the problem of interobserver agreement. Given the same result to interpret, two people will agree in only a proportion of cases, generally expressed as the κ score. If the test in question gives results in terms of numbers (such as the blood cholesterol concentration in mmol/L), interobserver agreement is hardly an issue. If, however, the test involves reading $x$ rays (such as the mammogram example in section 4.5) or asking people questions about their drinking habits[9], it is important to confirm that reproducibility between observers is at an acceptable level.

*Question 7—What are the features of the test as derived from this validation study?*

All the above standards could have been met but the test might still be worthless because the test itself is not valid—that is, its sensitivity, specificity, and other crucial features are too low. That is arguably the case for using urine glucose as a screening test for diabetes (see section 7.2 above). After all, if a test has a false negative rate of nearly 80%, it is more likely to mislead the clinician than assist the diagnosis if the target disorder is actually present.

There are no absolutes for the validity of a screening test, as what counts as acceptable depends on the condition being screened for. Few of us would quibble about a test for colour blindness that was 95% sensitive and 80% specific, but nobody ever died of colour blindness. The Guthrie heel prick screening test for congenital hypothyroidism, performed on all babies in the UK soon after birth, is over 99% sensitive but has a positive predictive value of only 6% (in other words, it picks up almost all babies with the condition at the expense of a high false positive rate)[10], and rightly so. It is far more important to pick up every single baby with this treatable condition, who would otherwise develop severe mental handicap, than to save hundreds of parents the relatively minor stress of a repeat blood test on their baby.

*Question 8—Were confidence intervals given for sensitivity, specificity, and other features of the test?*

As section 5.5 explained, a confidence interval, which can be calculated for virtually every numerical aspect of a set of results, expresses the possible range of results within which the true value lies. Go back to the jury example in section 7.1. If they had found just one more murderer not guilty, the sensitivity of their verdict would have gone down from 67% to 33% and the positive predictive value of the verdict from 33% to 20%. This enormous (and quite unacceptable) sensitivity to a single case decision is, of course, because we validated the jury's performance on only ten cases. The confidence intervals for the features of this jury are so wide that my computer programme refuses to calculate them! Remember, the larger the sample size, the narrower the confidence interval, so it is particularly important to look for confidence intervals if the paper you are reading reports a study on a relatively small sample. If you would like the formula for calculating confidence intervals for diagnostic test features, see Gardner and Altman's textbook *Statistics with Confidence*[11].

*Question 9—Has a sensible "normal range" been derived from these results?*

If the test gives non-dichotomous (continuous) results—that is, if it gives a numerical value rather than a yes/no result—someone will have to say at what value the test result will count as abnormal. Many of us have been there with our own blood pressure reading.

We want to know if our result is "okay" or not, but the doctor insists on giving us a value such as "142/92". If 140/90 were chosen as the cutoff for high blood pressure, we would be placed in the "abnormal" category, even though our risk of adverse outcome is hardly different from that of a person with a blood pressure of 138/88. Quite sensibly, many practising doctors advise their patients, "Your blood pressure isn't quite right, but it doesn't fall into the danger zone. Come back in three months for another check". Nevertheless, the doctor must at some stage make the decision that *this* blood pressure needs treating with tablets but *that* one does not.

Defining relative and absolute danger zones for a continuous physiological or pathological variable is a complex science, which should take into account the actual likelihood of the adverse outcome that the proposed treatment aims to prevent. This process is made considerably more objective by the use of likelihood ratios (see section 7.4). For an entertaining discussion on the different possible meanings of the word "normal" in diagnostic investigations, see Sackett and colleagues' textbook[6], page 59.

*Question 10—Has this test been placed in the context of other potential tests in the diagnostic sequence for the condition?*

In general, we treat high blood pressure simply on the basis of the blood pressure reading alone (although we tend to rely on a series of readings rather than a single value). Compare this with the sequence we use to diagnose stenosis ("hardening") of the coronary arteries. Firstly, we select patients with a typical history of effort angina (chest pain on exercise). Next, we usually do a resting electrocardiogram, an exercise electrocardiogram, and, in some cases, a radionucleide scan of the heart to look for areas short of oxygen. Most patients come to a coronary angiogram (the definitive investigation for coronary artery stenosis) only *after* they have produced an abnormal result on these preliminary tests.

If you took 100 people off the street and sent them straight for a coronary angiogram, the test might display very different positive and negative predictive values (and even different sensitivity and specificity) than it did in the sicker population on which it was originally validated. This means that the various aspects of validity of the coronary angiogram as a diagnostic test are virtually meaningless unless these figures are expressed in terms of what they contribute to the overall diagnostic work up.

## 7.4 A note on likelihood ratios

Question 9 above described the problem of defining a normal range for a continuous variable. In such circumstances it can be preferable to express the test result not as "normal" or "abnormal" but in terms of the actual chances of a patient having the target disorder if the test result reaches a particular level. Take, for example, the use of the prostate specific antigen (PSA) test to screen for prostate cancer. Most men will have some detectable PSA in their blood (say, 0.5 ng/ml), and most of those with advanced prostate cancer will have very high concentrations of PSA (above about 20 ng/ml). But a concentration of, say, 7.4 ng/ml may be found either in a perfectly normal man or in someone with early cancer. There simply is not a clean cut off between normal and abnormal[12].

We can, however, use the results of a validation study of the PSA test against a gold standard for prostate cancer (say a biopsy) to draw up a whole series of two by two tables. Each table would use a different definition of an abnormal PSA result to classify patients as "normal" or "abnormal". From these tables, we could generate different likelihood ratios associated with a concentration above each different cut off point. Then, when faced with a result in the "grey zone", we would at least be able to say, "this test has not proved that the patient has prostate cancer, but it has increased [or decreased] the likelihood of that diagnosis by a factor of $x$".

Although the likelihood ratio is one of the more complicated aspects of a diagnostic test to calculate, it has enormous practical value and it is becoming the preferred way of expressing and comparing the usefulness of different tests. As Sackett and colleagues explain at great length in their textbook[6], the likelihood ratio can be used directly in ruling a particular diagnosis in or out. For example, if a person enters my consulting room with no symptoms at all, I know that they have a 5% chance of having iron deficiency anaemia since I know that one person in 20 in the population has this condition (in the language of diagnostic tests, this means that the pretest probability of anaemia, equivalent to the prevalence of the condition, is 0.05)[13].

Now, if I do a diagnostic test for anaemia—the serum ferritin concentration—the result will usually make the diagnosis of anaemia either more or less likely. A moderately reduced serum ferritin concentration (between 18 and 45 µg/l) has a likelihood ratio of 3, so the chance of a patient with this result having iron deficiency anaemia is generally calculated to be 0.05 x 3—or 0.15 (15%). This value is known as the post-test probability of the serum ferritin test. Strictly speaking, likelihood ratios should be used on odds rather than probabilities, but the simpler method shown here gives a good approximation when the pre-test probability is low. In this example, a pre-test probability of 5% is equal to a pre-test odds of 0.5/0.95 or 0.053; a positive test with a likelihood ratio of 3 gives a post-test odds of 0.158, which is equal to a post-test probability of 14%.

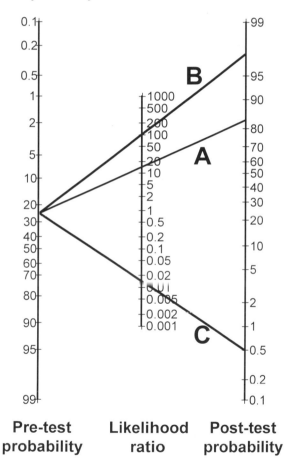

Fig 7.1 Using likelihood ratios to calculate the post-test probability of someone being a smoker

Figure 7.1 shows a nomogram, adapted by Sackett and colleagues from an original paper by Fagan[14], for working out post-test probabilities when the pretest probability (prevalence) and likelihood ratio for the test are known. The lines A, B, and C, drawn from a pretest probability of 25% (the prevalence of smoking among British adults) are, respectively, the trajectories through likelihood ratios of 15, 100, and 0.015—three different tests for detecting whether someone is a smoker[15]. Actually, test C detects whether the person is a *non-smoker* as a positive result in this test leads to a post-test probability of only 0.5%.

In summary, as I said at the beginning of this chapter, you can get a long way with diagnostic tests without referring to likelihood ratios. I avoided them myself for years. But if you put aside an afternoon to get to grips with this aspect of clinical epidemiology, I predict that your time will have been well spent.

1   WHO Study Group. Diabetes mellitus. *WHO Tech Rep Ser* 1985; **727**.
2   McCance DR, Hanson RL, Charles M-A, *et al*. Comparison of tests for glycated haemoglobin and fasting and two hour plasma glucose concentrations as diagnostic measures for diabetes. *BMJ* 1994; **308**: 1323-8.
3   Andersson DKG, Lundbld E, Svardsudd K. A model for early diagnosis of type 2 diabetes mellitus in primary health care. *Diabet Med* 1993; **10**: 167-73.
4   Jaeschke R, Guyatt G, Sackett DL. Users' guides to the medical literature. III. How to use an article about a diagnostic test. A. Are the results of the study valid? *JAMA* 1994; **271**: 389-91.
5   Jaeschke R, Guyatt G, Sackett DL. Users' guides to the medical literature. III. How to use an article about a diagnostic test. B. What were the results and will they help me in caring for my patients? *JAMA* 1994; **271**: 703-7.
6   Sackett DL, Haynes RB, Guyatt GH, *et al. Clinical epidemiology—a basic science for clinical medicine.* London: Little, Brown, 1991: 51-68.
7   Read MC, Lachs MS, Feinstein AR. Use of methodological standards in diagnostic test research: getting better but still not good. *JAMA* 1995; **274**: 645-51.
8   Mant D. Testing a test: three critical steps. In: Jones R, Kinmonth A-L, eds. *Critical reading for primary care.* Oxford: Oxford University Press, 1995: 183-90.
9   Bush B, Shaw S, Cleary P, *et al*. Screening for alcohol abuse using the CAGE questionnaire. *Am J Med* 1987; **82**: 231-6.
10  Verkerk PH, Derksen-Lubsen G, Vulsma T, *et al*. Evaluation of a decade of neonatal screening for congenital hypothyroidism in the Netherlands. *Nederlands Tijdschrift voor Geneeskunde* 1993; **137**: 2199-205.
11  Gardner MJ, Altman DG, eds. *Statistics with confidence: confidence intervals and statistical guidelines.* London: BMJ Publishing, 1989.
12  Catalona WJ, Hudson MA, Scardino PT, *et al*. Selection of optimal prostate specific antigen cutoffs for early diagnosis of prostate cancer: receiver operator characteristic curves. *J Urol* 1994; **152**: 2037-42.
13  Guyatt GH, Patterson C, Ali M, *et al*. Diagnosis of iron deficiency anemia in the elderly. *Am J Med* 1990; **88**: 205-9.
14  Fagan TJ. Nomogram for Bayes' theorem. *N Engl J Med* 1975; **293**: 257-61.
15  Anonymous. How good is that test—using the result. *Bandolier* 1996; **3**: 6-8.

# Chapter 8: Papers that summarise other papers (systematic reviews and meta-analyses)

## 8.1 When is a review systematic?

Remember the essays you used to write when you first started college? You would mooch round the library, browsing through the indexes of books and journals. When you came across a paragraph that looked relevant you copied it out, and if anything you found did not fit in with the theory you were proposing, you left it out. This, more or less, constitutes the methodology of the *narrative* review—an overview of primary studies that have not been identified or analysed in a systematic (that is, standardised and objective) way. Journalists, who get paid according to how much they write rather than how much they read or how critically they process it, take the narrative review to its most selective extreme, which explains why most of the "new scientific breakthroughs" you read in your newspaper today will probably be discredited before the year is out. In contrast, a *systematic review* is an overview of primary studies that

- Contains an explicit statement of objectives, materials, and methods

- Has been conducted according to explicit and reproducible methodology (see figure 8.1)[1]

The most enduring and useful systematic reviews, notably those undertaken by the Cochrane Collaboration (see section 2.10), are regularly updated to incorporate new evidence.

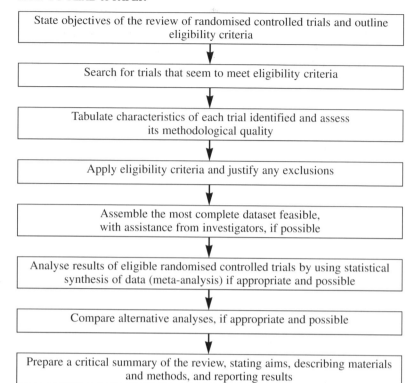

Figure 8.1: Methodology for a systematic review of randomised controlled trials

Many, if not most, medical review articles are still written in narrative or journalistic form. Professor Paul Knipschild, in Iain Chalmers and Douglas Altman's excellent book, *Systematic Reviews*[2], describes how Nobel prize winning biochemist Linus Pauling used selective quotes from the medical literature to "prove" his theory that vitamin C helps you live longer and feel better[3]. When Knipschild and his colleagues searched the literature *systematically* for evidence for and against this hypothesis, they found that, although one or two trials did strongly suggest that vitamin C could prevent the onset of the common cold, there were far more studies that did not show any beneficial effect.

Linus Pauling probably did not deliberately intend to deceive his readers, but since his enthusiasm for his espoused cause outweighed his scientific objectivity he was unaware of the *selection bias* influencing his choice of papers. Much work has been done,

112

most notably by Professor Cynthia Mulrow of the University of Texas Health Science Center, United States, which confirms the sneaky feeling that were you or I to attempt what Pauling did—that is, hunt through the medical literature for "evidence" to support our pet theory—we would make an equally idiosyncratic and unscientific job of it[4]. Mulrow, along with Iain Chalmers at the UK Cochrane Centre and Peter Gøtzsche and Andy Oxman of the Nordic Cochrane Centre (see section 2.10) deserves much of the credit for persuading the rest of the medical community that flawed secondary research, exemplified by the journalistic review, is as scientifically dangerous as flawed primary research. Some advantages of the systematic review are given in box 8.1.

---

### Box 8.1 Advantages of systematic reviews[3]

- Explicit methods *limit bias* in identifying and rejecting studies
- Conclusions are hence more *reliable* and *accurate*
- Large amounts of *information* can be assimilated quickly by health care providers, researchers, and policymakers
- Delay between research discoveries and *implementation* of effective diagnostic and therapeutic strategies is potentially reduced (see chapter 12)
- Results of different studies can be formally compared to establish *generalisability* of findings and *consistency* (lack of heterogeneity) of results (see section 8.4)
- Reasons for *heterogeneity* (inconsistency in results across studies) can be identified and new hypotheses generated about particular subgroups (see section 8.4)
- Quantitative systematic reviews (meta-analyses) increase the *precision* of the overall result (see sections 4.6 and 8.3)

---

Experts, who have been steeped in a subject for years and know what the answer "ought" to be, are significantly less able to produce an objective review of the literature in their subject than non-experts[5]. This would be of little consequence if experts' opinion could be relied on to be congruent with the results of independent systematic reviews, but they most certainly can't[6]. In other words, if you are going to pay someone to seek out the best objective evidence of the benefits of anticoagulants in atrial fibrillation, you should ask someone who is an expert in systematic reviews to work alongside an expert in atrial fibrillation.

I hope you have noticed that the procedure for systematic

review, outlined in figure 8.1, is an example of *deductive reasoning* (see section 3.1), in which the "data" (in this instance, the published trials) are collected in a manner that minimises bias, and the conclusions flow from what the data show. At any stage, new data could be produced that are inconsistent with the conclusion, which must then be rejected (or, at least, modified). In contrast, the journalistic review, illustrated by Pauling's book[3], is an excellent example of *inductive* reasoning in secondary research: when trials are found that fail to support the hypothesis it is the trials that get rejected rather than the hypothesis.

To be fair to Pauling, he did mention a number of trials whose results seriously challenged his theory that vitamin C prevents the common cold[3]. But he described all such trials as "methodologically flawed". As Knipschild reminds us, so were many of the trials that Pauling *did* include in his analysis but because their results were consistent with the theory, Pauling was, perhaps subconsciously, less critical of weaknesses in their design.

I mention this to illustrate the point that, when undertaking a systematic review, not only must the search for relevant articles be thorough and objective, but the criteria used to reject articles as "flawed" must be explicit and independent of the results of those trials. In other words, you don't trash a trial because all the other trials in this area showed something different (see section 8.4); you trash it because, *whatever the results showed*, the trial's objectives or methods did not meet your predefined standards.

## 8.2 Evaluating systematic reviews

*Question 1—Can you find an important clinical question that the review examined?*

Look back to chapter 3, in which I explained the importance of defining the question when you read a paper about a clinical trial or other form of primary research. I called this "getting your bearings" as one sure way to be confused about a paper is to fail to ascertain what it is about. The definition of a specific answerable question is, if anything, even more important (and even more commonly omitted) in the preparation of an overview of primary studies. If you have ever tried to put together the findings of a dozen or more clinical papers into an essay, editorial, or summary notes for an examination, you will know that it is all too easy to meander into aspects of the subject that you never intended to cover.

The question examined by a systematic review needs to be defined very precisely as the reviewer must make a dichotomous (yes/no) decision as to whether each potentially relevant paper will be included or, alternatively, rejected as "irrelevant". The question, "Do anticoagulants prevent strokes in patients with atrial fibrillation?" sounds pretty specific, until you start looking through the list of possible studies to include. Does "atrial fibrillation" include both rheumatic and non-rheumatic forms (which are known to be associated with very different risks of stroke), and does it include intermittent atrial fibrillation (my grandfather, for example, used to go into this arrhythmia for a few hours whenever he drank coffee and would have counted as a "grey case" in any trial)?

Does "stroke" include both ischaemic stroke (caused by a *blocked* blood vessel in the brain) and haemorrhagic stroke (caused by a *burst* blood vessel)? And, talking of burst blood vessels, shouldn't we be weighing the side effects of anticoagulants against their possible benefits? Should true anticoagulants such as heparin and warfarin be compared with placebo or should they be compared with other drugs that reduce the clotting tendency of the blood, such as aspirin and related products? Finally, should the review cover trials on patients who have already had a previous stroke or transient ischaemic attack (a mild stroke that gets better within 24 hours) or should it be limited to trials on patients without these major risk factors for a further stroke? The "simple" question posed earlier is becoming unanswerable, and we must refine it as follows:

"To assess the effectiveness and safety of warfarin type anticoagulant therapy in secondary prevention (that is, after a previous stroke or transient ischaemic attack) in patients with non-rheumatic atrial fibrillation: comparison with placebo"[7].

*Question 2—Was a thorough search done of the appropriate database(s) and were other potentially important sources explored?*

As figure 8.1 illustrates, one of the benefits of a systematic review is that, unlike a narrative or journalistic review, the author is required to tell you where the information in it came from and how it was processed. As I explained in chapter 2, searching the

115

Medline database for relevant articles is a very sophisticated science, and even the best Medline search will miss important papers, for which the reviewer must approach other databases such as listed in section 2.10.

In the search for trials to include in a review, the scrupulous avoidance of linguistic imperialism is a scientific as well as a political imperative. As much weight must be given, for example, to the expressions "Eine Placebo-kontrolierte Doppelblindstudie" and "une étude randomisée a double insu face au placebo" as to "a double blind, randomised controlled trial"[8]. Furthermore, particularly when a statistical synthesis of results (meta-analysis) is contemplated, it may be necessary to write and ask the authors of the primary studies for raw data on individual patients that were never included in the published review (see section 8.3).

---

**Box 8.2  Checklist of data sources for a systematic review**

- Medline database
- Cochrane controlled clinical trials register (see section 2.10)
- Other medical and paramedical databases (see section 2.10)
- Foreign language literature
- "Grey literature" (theses, internal reports, non-peer reviewed journals, pharmaceutical industry files)
- References (and references of references, etc) cited in primary sources
- Other unpublished sources known to experts in the specialty (seek by personal communication)
- Raw data from published trials (seek by personal communication)

---

As Paul Knipschild and his colleagues showed when they searched for trials on vitamin C and cold prevention, their electronic databases gave them only 22 of their final total of 61 trials. Another 39 trials were uncovered by hand searching the manual Index Medicus database (14 trials not identified previously) and searching the references of the trials identified in Medline (15 more trials), the references of the references (9 further trials), and the references of the references of the references (one additional trial not identified by any of the previous searches).

Do not be too hard on a reviewer, however, if he or she has not followed this counsel of perfection to the letter. After all, Knipschild and his team found that only one of the trials not identified in Medline met stringent criteria for methodological quality and ultimately contributed to their systematic review of vitamin C in cold prevention[8]. An exploration of non-Medline databases and "grey literature" (see box 8.2) may be of greater relative importance when trials outside the medical mainstream, such as physiotherapy or alternative medicine, are looked at[9].

*Question 3—Was methodological quality assessed and the trials weighted accordingly?*

Chapters 3 and 4 and appendix A provide some checklists for assessing whether a paper should be rejected outright on methodological grounds. But given that only around 1% of clinical trials are said to be beyond criticism in terms of methodology, the practical question is how to ensure that a "small but perfectly formed" study is given the weight it deserves in relation to a larger study whose methodology is adequate but more open to criticism.

Methodological shortcomings that invalidate the results of trials are often generic (that is, they are independent of the subject matter of the study; see appendix A), but there may also be particular methodological features that distinguish between good, medium,

---

**Box 8.3  Assigning weight to trials in a systematic review**

Each trial should be evaluated in terms of its
- *Methodological quality*—that is, extent to which the design and conduct are likely to have prevented systematic errors (bias) (see section 4.4)
- *Precision*—that is, a measure of the likelihood of random errors (usually depicted as the width of the confidence interval around the result)
- *External validity*—that is, the extent to which the results are generalisable or applicable to a particular target population

(Additional aspects of "quality" such as scientific importance, clinical importance, and literary quality, are rightly given great weight by peer reviewers and journal editors but are less relevant to the systematic reviewer once the question to be examined has been defined)

---

and poor quality in a particular field. Hence, one of the tasks of a systematic reviewer is to draw up a list of criteria, including both generic and particular aspects of quality, against which to judge each trial. In theory, a composite numerical score could be calculated that would reflect overall methodological quality. In reality, however, care should be taken in the development of such scores as there is no gold standard for the "true" methodological quality of a trial[10] and such composite scores are probably neither valid nor reliable in practice[11 12]. The various Cochrane Collaborative Review Groups are in the process of developing topic-specific methodology for assigning quality scores to research studies[13 14].

*Question 4—How sensitive are the results to the way the review has been done?*

If you don't understand what this question means, look up the tongue in cheek paper by Carl Counsell and colleagues in the Christmas 1994 issue of the *British Medical Journal,* which "proved" an entirely spurious relation between the result of shaking a dice and the outcome of an acute stroke[15]. The authors report a series of artificial dice rolling experiments in which red, white, and green dice, respectively, represented different treatments for acute stroke.

Overall, the "trials" showed no significant benefit from the three treatments. However, the simulation of a number of perfectly plausible events if the process of meta-analysis—such as the exclusion of several of the "negative" trials through publication bias (see section 3.3), a subgroup analysis that excluded data on red dice treatment (since, on looking back at the results, red dice seemed to be harmful), and other, essentially arbitrary, exclusions on the grounds of "methodological quality"—led to an apparently highly significant benefit of "dice treatment" in acute stroke.

You cannot, of course, cure anyone of a stroke by rolling a dice, but if these simulated results pertained to a genuine medical controversy (such as which groups of postmenopausal women should take hormone replacement therapy or whether breech babies should routinely be delivered by caesarean section) how would you spot these subtle biases? The answer is you need to work through the "what ifs". What if the authors of the systematic review had changed the inclusion criteria for studies? What if they had excluded unpublished studies? What if their "quality weightings" had been assigned differently? What if trials of lower methodological quality had been included (or excluded)? What if all the unaccounted for patients in each trial were assumed to have died (or been cured)?

An exploration of what ifs is known as a *sensitivity analysis*. If you find that fiddling with the data like this in various ways makes little or no difference to the review's overall results, you can assume that its conclusions are relatively robust. If, however, the key findings disappear when any of the what ifs changes, the conclusions should be expressed far more cautiously and you should hesitate before changing your practice in the light of them.

*Question 5—Have the numerical results been interpreted with common sense and due regard to the broader aspects of the problem?*

As the next section shows, it is easy to be phased by the figures and graphs in a systematic review. But any numerical result, however precise, accurate, "significant", or otherwise incontrovertible, must be placed in the context of the painfully simple and (often) frustratingly general question that the review examined. The clinician must decide how (if at all) this numerical result, *whether significant or not*, should influence the care of an individual patient.

A particularly important feature to consider when undertaking or appraising a systematic review is the external validity of included trials (see box 8.3). A trial may be of high methodological quality and have a precise and numerically impressive result, but it may, for example, have been conducted on participants under the age of 60 and hence will not be valid for people over 75. The inclusion in systematic reviews of irrelevant studies is guaranteed to lead to absurdities and reduce the credibility of secondary research, as Sir John Grimley Evans argued recently (see section 9.1)[16].

## 8.3 Meta-analysis for the non-statistician

If I had to pick one word that exemplifies the fear and loathing felt by so many students, clinicians, and consumers towards evidence based medicine, that word would be "meta-analysis". The meta-analysis, defined as *a statistical synthesis of the numerical results of several trials that all examined the same question,* is the statistician's chance to pull a double whammy on you. Firstly, they phase you with all the statistical tests in the individual papers and then they

119

use a whole new battery of tests to produce a new set of odds ratios, confidence intervals, and values for significance.

As I confessed in chapter 5, I, too, tend to go into panic mode at the sight of ratios, square root signs, and half forgotten Greek letters. But before you consign meta-analysis to the set of newfangled techniques that you will never understand, remember two things. Firstly, the meta-analyst may wear an anorak but he or she is *on your side*. A good meta-analysis is often easier for the non-statistician to understand than the stack of primary research papers from which it was derived, for reasons that I am about to explain. Secondly, the underlying statistical techniques used for meta-analysis are exactly the same as the ones for any other data analysis—it's just that some of the numbers are bigger.

The first task of the meta-analyst, after following the preliminary steps for systematic review in figure 8.1, is to decide which out of all the various outcome measures chosen by the authors of the primary studies is the best one (or ones) to use in the overall synthesis. In trials of a particular chemotherapy regimen for breast cancer, for example, some authors will have published cumulative mortality figures (that is, the total number of people who have died to date) at   cut off points of three and twelve months, whereas other trials will have published six month, twelve month, and five year cumulative mortality. The meta-analyst might decide to concentrate on twelve month mortality because this result can be easily extracted from all the papers. He or she may, however, decide that three month mortality is a clinically important end point and would need to write to the authors of the remaining trials asking for the raw data from which to calculate these figures.

In addition to crunching the numbers, part of the meta-analyst's job description is to tabulate relevant information on the inclusion criteria, sample size, characteristics of patients at baseline, withdrawal rate, and results of primary and secondary end points of all the studies included. If this task has been done properly, you will be able to compare both the methodology and the results of two trials whose authors wrote up their research in different ways. Although such tables are often visually daunting, they save you having to plough through the methods sections of each paper and compare one author's tabulated results with another author's pie chart or histogram.

These days, the results of meta-analyses tend to be presented in a fairly standard form. This is partly because meta-analysts often use computer software (most commonly MetaView, which is the package used by the UK Cochrane Centre) to do the calculations for them, and this includes a standard graphics package that presents results as illustrated in figure 8.2. I have reproduced in MetaView (with the authors' permission) this pictorial representation (colloquially known as a "forest plot" or "blobbogram") of the pooled odds ratios of eight randomised controlled trials that each compared coronary artery bypass graft (CABG) with percutaneous coronary angioplasty (PTCA) in the treatment of severe angina[17]. The primary (main) outcome in this meta-analysis was death or heart attack within one year.

The eight trials, each represented by its acronym (for example, CABRI) are listed, one below the other on the left hand side of the figure. The horizontal line corresponding to each trial shows the relative risk of death or heart attack at one year in patients randomised to PTCA compared with patients randomised to CABG. The "blob" in the middle of each line is the point estimate of the difference between the groups (the best single estimate of the benefit in lives saved by offering CABG rather than PTCA) and the width of the line represents the 95% confidence interval of this estimate (see p 81). The black line down the middle of the picture is known as the "line of no effect" and in this case is associated with a relative risk (RR) of 1.0. In other words, if the horizontal line for any trial does not cross the line of no effect, there is a 95% chance that there is a "real" difference between the groups.

As sections 4.6 and 5.5 argued, if the confidence interval of the result (the horizontal line) *does* cross the line of no effect (that is, the vertical line) that can mean *either* that there is no significant difference between the treatments *or* that the sample size was too small to allow us to be confident where the true result lies, *or both*. The various individual studies give point estimates of the relative risk of PTCA compared with CABG of between about 0.5 and 5.0, and the confidence intervals of some studies are so wide that they don't even fit on the graph.

Now, here comes the fun of meta-analysis. Look at the diamond below all the horizontal lines. This represents the *pooled* data from all eight trials (overall relative risk PTCA:CABG = 1.08), with a new, much narrower, confidence interval of this relative risk (0.79 to 1.50). Since the diamond firmly overlaps the line of no effect, we can say that there is probably little to choose between the two

121

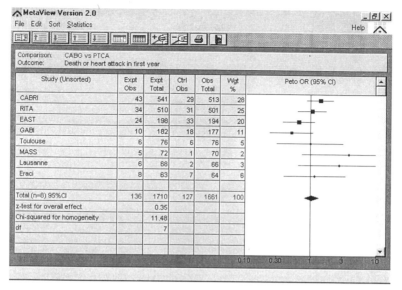

Figure 8.2 Pooled odds ratios of eight randomised controlled trials of coronary artery bypass graft against percutaneous coronary angiography, shown in MetaView format

treatments in terms of the primary end point (death or heart attack in the first year). Now, in this example, every single one of the eight trials also suggested a non-significant effect, but in none of them was the sample size large enough for us to be *confident* in that negative result.

Note, however, that this neat little diamond does *not* mean that you might as well offer PTCA rather than a CABG to every patient with angina. It has a much more limited meaning—that the *average* patient in the trials presented in this meta-analysis is equally likely to encounter the primary outcome (death or heart attack within a year) whichever of these two treatments they were randomised to receive. If you read the paper by Pocock and colleagues[17], you would find important differences in the groups in terms of prevalence of angina and requirement for further operative intervention after the initial procedure. The choice of treatment should also, of course, take into account how the patient feels about undergoing major heart surgery (CABG) as opposed to the relatively minor procedure of PTCA.

**THE COCHRANE
COLLABORATION**

Figure 8.3
Cochrane Collaboration Logo

In many meta-analyses, "non-significant" trials (that is, ones that, on their own, did not demonstrate a significant difference between treatment and control groups) contribute to a pooled result that *is* statistically significant. The most famous example of this, which the Cochrane Collaboration adopted as its logo (figure 8.3), is the meta-analysis of seven trials of the effect of giving steroids to mothers who were expected to give birth prematurely. Only two of the seven trials showed a statistically significant benefit (in terms of survival of the infant), but the improvement in precision (that is, the narrowing of confidence intervals) in the pooled results, shown by the narrower width of the diamond compared with the individual lines, demonstrates the strength of the evidence in favour of this intervention. This meta-analysis showed that infants of mothers treated with steroids were 30% to 50% less likely to die than infants of control mothers. This example is discussed further in section 12.1 in relation to changing clinicians' behaviour.

If you have followed the arguments on meta-analysis of published trial results this far, you might like to read up on the more sophisticated technique of meta-analysis of individual patient data, which provides a more accurate and precise figure for the point estimate of effect[18].

## 8.4 Explaining heterogeneity

In everyday language, "homogeneous" means "of uniform composition" and "heterogeneous" means "many different ingredients". In the language of meta-analysis, homogeneity means

123

that the results of each individual trial are compatible with the results of any of the others. Homogeneity can be estimated at a glance once the trial results have been presented in the format illustrated in figures 8.2 and 8.4. In figure 8.2, the lower confidence limit of every trial is below the upper confidence limit of all the others (that is, the horizontal lines all overlap to some extent). Statistically speaking, the trials are homogeneous. Conversely, in figure 8.4 (which is discussed further below) there are some trials whose lower confidence limit is above the upper confidence limit of one or more other trials (that is, some lines do not overlap at all). These trials may be said to be heterogeneous.

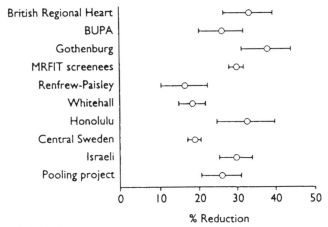

Figure 8.4 Reduction in risk of heart disease by strategies to lower cholesterol concentration[19]

You may have spotted by now (particularly if you have already read section 5.5 on confidence intervals) that pronouncing a set of trials heterogeneous on the basis of whether their confidence intervals overlap is somewhat arbitrary as the confidence interval itself is arbitrary (it can be set at 90%, 95%, 99%, or indeed any other value). The definitive test entails a slightly more sophisticated statistical manoeuvre than holding a ruler up against the blobbogram. The one most commonly used is a variant of the $\chi^2$ test (see table 5.1, p 73), as the question examined is, "Is there greater variation between the results of the trials than is compatible with the play of chance?"

The $\chi^2$ statistic for heterogeneity is explained in more detail by Simon Thompson[19], who offers the following useful rule of thumb: a $\chi^2$ statistic has, on average, a value equal to its degrees of freedom (in this case, the number of trials in the meta-analysis minus one), so a $\chi^2$ of 7.0 for a set of 8 trials would provide no evidence of statistical heterogeneity. (In fact, it would not prove that the trials were homogeneous either, particularly since the $\chi^2$ test has low power (see section 4.6) to detect small but important levels of heterogeneity.)

A $\chi^2$ value much greater than the number of trials in a meta-analysis tells us that the trials that contributed to the analysis are different in some important way from one another. There may, for example, be known differences in methodology (for example, authors may have used different questionnaires to assess the symptoms of depression) or known clinical differences in the trial participants (for example, one centre might have been a tertiary referral hospital to which all the sickest patients were referred). There may, however, be unknown or unrecorded differences between the trials that the meta-analyst can only speculate on until he or she has extracted further details from the trials' authors. Remember: demonstrating statistical heterogeneity is a mathematical exercise and is the job of the statistician but explaining this heterogeneity (that is, looking for, and accounting for, *clinical* heterogeneity) is an interpretive exercise and requires imagination, common sense, and hands on clinical or research experience.

Figure 8.4, which is reproduced with permission from Simon Thompson's chapter on the subject[19], shows the results of ten trials of cholesterol lowering strategies. The results are expressed as the percentage reduction in risk of heart disease associated with each 0.6 mmol/l reduction in serum cholesterol concentration. The horizontal lines represent the 95% confidence intervals of each result, and it is clear, even without being told the $\chi^2$ statistic of 127, that the trials are highly heterogeneous.

Simply to "average out" the results of the trials in figure 8.4 would be very misleading. The meta-analyst must return to his or her primary sources and ask, "In what way was trial A different from trial B, and what do trials C, D, and H have in common that makes their results cluster at one extreme of the figure?" In this example, a correction for the age of the trial subjects reduced $\chi^2$ from 127 to 45. In other words, most of the "incompatibility" in the results of these trials can be explained by the fact that by embarking on a strategy (such as a special diet) that successfully reduces your cholesterol concentration you will be substantially more likely to prevent a heart attack if you are 45 than if you are 85.

This, essentially, is the essence of the grievance of Professor Hans Eysenck, who has constructed a vigorous and entertaining critique of the science of meta-analysis[20]. In a world of lumpers and splitters, Eysenck is a splitter, and it offends his sense of the qualitative and the particular (see chapter 11) to combine the results of studies that were done on different populations in different places at different times and for different reasons.

Eysenck's reservations about meta-analysis are borne out in the infamously discredited meta-analysis that demonstrated (wrongly) that there was significant benefit to be had from giving intravenous magnesium to heart attack victims. A subsequent megatrial involving 58 000 patients (ISIS-4) failed to find any benefit whatsoever, and the meta-analysts' misleading conclusions were subsequently explained in terms of publication bias, methodological weaknesses in the smaller trials, and clinical heterogeneity[21 22].

Although Eysenck's mathematical naivety is embarrasing ("if a medical treatment has an effect so recondite and obscure as to require a meta-analysis to establish it, I would not be happy to have it used on me"), I have a great deal of sympathy for the body of his argument. As one who tends to side with the splitters, I would put Eysenck's misgivings about meta-analysis high on the list of required reading for the aspiring systematic reviewer.

[1] Cochrane Collaboration Handbook [updated 9 December 1996]. Available in the Cochrane Library [database on disk and CD ROM]. The Cochrane Collaboration; Issue 1. Oxford: Update Software; 1997.

[2] Chalmers I, Altman DG, eds. *Systematic reviews.* London: BMJ Publishing, 1995.

[3] Pauling L. *How to live longer and feel better.* New York: Freeman, 1986.

[4] Mulrow C. The medical review article: state of the science. *Ann Intern Med* 1987; **106**: 485-8.

[5] Oxman Ad, Guyatt GH. The science of reviewing research. *Ann NY Acad Sci* 1993; **703**: 125-31.

[6] Antman EM, Lau J, Kupelnick B, *et al.* A comparison of results of meta-analyses of randomised controlled trials and recommendations of clinical experts. *JAMA* 1992; **268**: 240-8.

[7] Koudstaal P. *Secondary prevention following stroke or TIA in patients with non-rheumatic atrial fibrillation: anticoagulant therapy versus control.* Oxford: The Cochrane Collaboration, 1995. (Cochrane Database of Systematic Reviews, updated 14 February 1995.)

[8] Knipschild P. Some examples of systematic reviews. In: Chalmers I, Altman DG, eds. *Systematic reviews*. London: BMJ Publishing, 1995: 9-16.

[9] Knipschild P. Searching for alternatives: loser pays. *Lancet* 1993; **341**: 1135-6.

[10] Oxman A, ed. *Preparing and maintaining systematic reviews*. Oxford: The Cochrane Collaboration, 1995. (In: Cochrane Collaboration Handbook, section VI, updated 14 July 1995.)

[11] Emerson JD, Burdick E, Hoaglin DC, *et al.* An empirical study of the possible relation of treatment differences to quality scores in controlled randomized clinical trials. *Cont Clin Trials* 1990; **11**: 339-52.

[12] Moher D, Jadad AR, Tugwell P. Assessing the quality of randomized controlled trials: current issues and future directions. *Int J Health Technol Assess* 1996; **12**: 195-208.

[13] Bero L, Rennie D. The Cochrane Collaboration: preparing, maintaining, and disseminating systematic reviews of the effects of health care. *JAMA* 1995; **274**: 1935-8.

[14] Garner P, Hetherington J. *Establishing and supporting collaborative review groups*. Oxford: The Cochrane Collaboration, 1995. (In: Cochrane Collaboration Handbook, section II, updated 14 July 1995.)

[15] Counsell CE, Clarke MJ, Slattery J, *et al.* The miracle of DICE therapy for acute stroke: fact or fictional product of subgroup analysis? *BMJ* 1994; **309**: 1677-81.

[16] Grimley Evans J. Evidence-based and evidence-biased medicine. *Age Aging* 1995; **24**: 461-3.

[17] Pocock SJ, Henderson RA, Rickards AF, *et al.* Meta-analysis of randomised trials comparing coronary angioplasty with bypass surgery. *Lancet* 1995; **346**: 1184-9.

[18] Clarke MJ, Stewart LA. Obtaining data from randomised controlled trials: How much do we need for reliable and informative meta-analyses? In: Chalmers I, Altman DG, eds. *Systematic reviews*. London: BMJ Publishing, 1995: 37-47.

[19] Thompson SG. Why sources of heterogeneity in meta-analysis should be investigated. In: Chalmers I, Altman DG, eds. *Systematic reviews*. London: BMJ Publishing, 1995: 48-63.

[20] Eysenck HJ. Problems with meta-analysis. In: Chalmers I, Altman DG, eds. *Systematic reviews*. London: BMJ Publishing, 1995: 64-74.

[21] Anon. Magnesium, myocardial infarction, meta-analysis and mega-trials. *Drug Ther Bull* 1995; **33**: 25-7.

[22] Egger M, Davey Smith G. Misleading meta-analysis (letter). *BMJ* 1995; **311**: 753-4.

# Chapter 9: Papers that tell you what to do (guidelines)

## 9.1 The great guidelines debate

Never was the chasm between clinicians and health service managers wider than in their respective attitudes to clinical guidelines. Managers (by which I include politicians and all those who help to implement, administer, evaluate, and finance the actions of clinicians but who do not themselves see patients) love guidelines. Clinicians, save for the important minority who actually write them, usually have a strong aversion to guidelines.

Before we carry this political hot potato any further, we need a definition of guidelines, for which the following will suffice:

> "Guidelines are systematically developed statements to assist practitioner decisions about appropriate health care for specific clinical circumstances."[1]

The purposes that guidelines serve are given in box 9.1. The image of the medical buffoon blundering blithely through the outpatient clinic still diagnosing the same illnesses and prescribing the same drugs he (or she) learnt about at medical school forty years previously and never having read a paper since knocks the "clinical freedom" argument (that is, that a doctor's professional opinion is beyond reproach) right out of the arena. Such hypothetical situations are grist to the mill of those who would impose "expert guidelines" on most if not all medical practice and hold to account all those who fail to keep in step.

But the counter argument to the excessive use, and particularly the compulsive imposition, of clinical guidelines is a powerful one,

## Box 9.1  Purpose of guidelines

- To make evidence based standards explicit and accessible (but see below—few guidelines currently in circulation are truly evidence based)
- To make decision making in the clinic and at the bedside easier and more objective
- To provide a yardstick for assessing professional performance
- To delineate the division of labour (for example, between GPs and consultants)
- To educate patients and professionals about current best practice
- To improve the cost-effectiveness of health services
- To serve as a tool for external control

and it has been expressed very eloquently by Professor J Grimley Evans:

"There is a fear that in the absence of evidence clearly applicable to the case in the hand a clinician might be forced by guidelines to make use of evidence which is only doubtfully relevant, generated perhaps in a different grouping of patients in another country at some other time and using a similar but not identical treatment. This is evidence-*biased* medicine; it is to use evidence in the manner of the fabled drunkard who searched under the street lamp for his door key because that is where the light was, even though he had dropped the key somewhere else"[3].

Grimley Evans' fear, which every practising clinician shares but few can articulate, is that politicians and health service managers who have jumped on the evidence based medicine bandwagon will use guidelines to decree the treatment of diseases rather than of patients. They will, it is feared, make judgments about people and their illnesses subservient to published evidence that an intervention is effective "on average". This, and other real and perceived disadvantages of guidelines are given in box 9.2, which has been compiled from a number of sources[3-9].

While the medicolegal implications of "official" guidelines have rarely been tested in the UK, courts in the United States have ruled that guideline developers can be held liable for faulty guidelines but that doctors cannot pass off their liability for poor clinical performance by claiming that adherence to guidelines corrupted their judgment[4].

129

---

**Box 9.2    Drawbacks of guidelines (real and perceived)**

- Guidelines may be intellectually suspect and reflect "expert opinion", which may formalise unsound practice
- By reducing medical practice variation they may standardise to "average" rather than best practice
- They inhibit innovation and prevent individual cases from being dealt with discretely and sensitively
- They could, theoretically, be used medicolegally (both in and out of context) to dictate what a competent practitioner "would have done" in particular circumstances
- Guidelines developed at national or regional level may not reflect local needs or have the ownership of local practitioners
- Guidelines developed in secondary care may not reflect demographic, clinical, or practical differences between this sector and the primary care setting
- Guidelines may produce undesirable shifts in the balance of power between different professional groups (for example, between clinicians and academics or purchasers and providers); hence, guideline development may be perceived as a political act

---

## 9.2  Do guidelines change clinicians' behaviour?

A systematic review of randomised trials and "other robust designs" by Grimshaw and Russell[10] demonstrated that *in the research setting* (in which participants were probably highly selected and evaluation was an explicit part of guideline introduction) all but four of 59 published studies demonstrated improvements— that is, changes in line with the guideline recommendations—in the process of care (what doctors did) and all but two of the eleven studies that measured outcome (what happened to the patients) reported significant improvements.

Grimshaw and Russell would be the first to emphasise, however, that despite these findings, guidelines do not necessarily improve either performance or outcome. Both they[10] and others[11] found wide variation in the size of the improvements in performance achieved by clinical guidelines. Grimshaw and Russell concluded that the probability of a guideline being effective depended on three factors, which are summarised in table 9.1: the development strategy (where and how the guidelines were produced), the

Table 9.1 Classification of clinical guidelines in terms of probability of being effective (after Grimshaw and Russell[10])

| Probability of being effective | Development strategy | Dissemination strategy | Implementation strategy |
| --- | --- | --- | --- |
| **High** | Internal | Specific educational intervention (for example, problem based learning package) | Patient specific reminder at time of consultation |
| **Above average** | Intermediate | Continuing education (for example, lecture) | Patient specific feedback |
| **Below average** | External, local | Mailing targeted groups | General feedback |
| **Low** | External, national | Publication in journal | General reminder |

dissemination strategy (how they were brought to the attention of clinicians), and the implementation strategy (how the clinician was prompted to follow them).

Table 9.1, in a nutshell, tells us that the most effective guidelines are developed locally by the people who are going to use them, introduced as part of a specific educational intervention, and implemented through a patient specific prompt that appears at the time of the consultation.

Subsequent publications have identified several barriers to the adoption of guidelines in practice[6-12]. These include:

- (Apparent) disagreements among experts about the quality of evidence *("Well, if they can't agree among themselves...")*

- Lack of appreciation of evidence by practitioners *("That's all very well, but when I trained we were always taught to hold back on steroids for asthma")*

- Defensive medicine *("I'll check all the tests anyway—belt and braces")*

- Strategic and cost constraints *("We can't afford to replace the equipment")*

- Specific practical constraints *("Where on earth did I put those guidelines?")*

131

- Failure of patients to accept procedures *("Mrs Brown insists she only needs a smear every five years")*

- Competing influences of other non-medical factors *("When we get the new computer system up and running...")*

- Lack of appropriate, patient specific feedback on performance *("I think I'm treating this condition OK")*

For a more detailed discussion on the barriers to implementing guidelines see Grimshaw and Russell's comprehensive discussion of the subject[13] and original research by other writers[11 14 15]. The successful introduction of guidelines needs "careful attention to the principles of change management: in particular...leadership, energy, avoidance of unnecessary uncertainty, good communication, and, above all, time"[8].

## 9.3    Questions to ask about a set of published guidelines

Like all published articles, guidelines would be easier to evaluate if they were presented in a standardised format. Box 9.3

---

**Box 9.3  Proposed format for structured abstracts of clinical practice guidelines[16]**

- *Objective*—The primary objective of the guideline, including the health problem and the targeted patients, providers, and settings
- *Options*—The clinical practice options considered in formulating the guideline
- *Outcomes*—Significant health and economic outcomes considered in comparing alternative practices
- *Evidence*—How and when evidence was gathered, selected, and synthesised
- *Values*—Disclosure of how values were assigned to potential outcomes of practice options and who participated in the process
- *Benefits, harms, and costs*—The type and magnitude of benefits, harms, and costs expected for patients from guideline implementation
- *Recommendations*—Summary of key recommendations
- *Validation*—Report of any external review, comparison with other guidelines, or clinical testing of guideline use
- *Sponsors*—Disclosure of the people who developed, funded, or endorsed the guideline

---

reproduces a suggested structured abstract for clinical guidelines[16]. But since few published guidelines currently follow such a format, you will probably have to scan the full text for answers to the questions below. In preparing the list that follows I have drawn on a number of previously published checklists and discussion documents[8 11 12 14 17-19].

*Question 1—Did the preparation and publication of these guidelines entail significant conflict of interest?*

I will resist labouring the point but a drug company that makes hormone replacement therapy or a research professor whose life's work has been spent perfecting this treatment might be tempted to recommend it for wider indications than the average clinician.

*Question 2—Are the guidelines concerned with an appropriate topic and do they state clearly the goal of ideal treatment in terms of health and/or cost outcome?*

Key questions in relation to choice of topic, reproduced from a recent article in the *British Medical Journal*[14], are given in box 9.4.

---

**Box 9.4  Key questions on choice of topic for guideline development[14]**

- Is the topic high volume, high risk, high cost?
- Are there large or unexplained variations in practice?
- Is the topic important in terms of the process and outcome of patient care?
- Is there potential for improvement?
- Is the investment of time and money likely to be repaid?
- Is the topic likely to hold the interest of team members?
- Is consensus likely?
- Will change benefit patients?
- Can change be implemented?

---

A guideline that says "do this" without telling the practitioner why such an action is desirable is bad psychology as well as poor science. The intended outcome if the guideline is followed might be better patient survival, lower complication rates, increased patient satisfaction, or savings in direct or indirect costs (see section 10.2). Whatever it is, it would be nice to know.

*Question 3—Was the guideline development panel headed by a leading expert in the field and was a specialist in the methodology of secondary research (for example, meta-analyst, health economist) involved?*

If a set of guidelines has been prepared entirely by a panel of internal "experts" you should, paradoxically, look at them particularly critically as researchers have been shown to be less objective in appraising evidence in their own speciality than in someone else's[20]. The involvement of an outsider (an expert in guideline development rather than in the particular clinical topic) to act as arbiter and methodological adviser will, hopefully, make the process more objective.

*Question 4—Have all the relevant data been scrutinised and do the guidelines' conclusions seem to be in keeping with the data?*

On the most basic level, was the literature analysed at all or are these guidelines simply a statement of the preferred practice of a selected panel of experts (that is, consensus guidelines)? If the literature was looked at, was a systematic search done and, if so, did it follow the methodology described in section 8.2? Were all papers unearthed by the search included or was an explicit scoring system used to reject those of poor methodological quality and give those of high quality the extra weight they deserved? In many cases, a search for rigorous and relevant research on which to base guidelines proves fruitless and the authors, unavoidably, resort to "best available" evidence or expert opinion.

*Question 5—Do the guidelines deal with variations in medical practice and other controversial areas (for example, optimum care in response to genuine or perceived underfunding)?*

It would be foolish to make dogmatic statements about ideal practice without reference to what actually goes on in the real world. There are many instances when some practitioners are marching to an altogether different tune from the rest of us (see section 1.2), and a good guideline should face such realities head on rather than hoping that the misguided minority will fall into step by default.

Another thorny issue that guidelines should tackle head on is where essential compromises should be made if financial constraints preclude "ideal" practice. If the ideal, for example, is to offer all patients with severe coronary artery disease a bypass operation (at the time of writing it isn't, but never mind) and the health service can afford to fund only 20% of such procedures, who should be pushed to the front of the queue?

*Question 6—Are the guidelines valid and reliable?*

In other words, can you trust them, and if a different guideline development panel examined the same question would they come up with the same guidelines? These, of course, are the two $64 000 questions. The academic validity of guidelines depends on whether they are supported by high quality research studies and on how strong the evidence from those studies is. In particular, issues of probability and confidence should have been dealt with acceptably (see section 4.6 and 5.5).

*Question 7—Are the guidelines clinically relevant, comprehensive, and flexible?*

In other words, are they written from the perspective of the practising doctor, nurse, midwife, physiotherapist, and so on, and do they take account of the type of patients he or she is likely to see, and in what circumstances? Perhaps the most common source of trouble here is when guidelines developed in secondary care and intended for use in hospital outpatients (who tend to be at the sicker end of the clinical spectrum) are passed on to the primary health care team with the intention of their being used in the primary care setting, where, in general, patients are less ill and may well need fewer investigations and less aggressive management. This issue is discussed in section 7.2 in relation to the different utility of diagnostic and screening tests in different populations.

Guidelines should cover all, or most, clinical eventualities. What if the patient is intolerant of the recommended medication? What if you can't send off all the recommended blood tests? What if the patient is very young, very old, or suffers from a coexisting illness? These, after all, are the patients who prompt most of us to reach for our guidelines, while the more "typical" patient tends to be managed without recourse to written instructions.

Flexibility is a particularly important consideration for national and regional bodies who set themselves up to develop guidelines. It has been repeatedly demonstrated that the ownership of guidelines by the people who are intended to use them locally is crucial to whether or not the guidelines are actually used[6 7 10]. If

135

there is no free rein for practitioners to adapt them to meet local needs and priorities, a set of guidelines will probably never get taken out of the drawer.

*Question 8—Do the guidelines take into account what is acceptable to, affordable by, and practically possible for patients?*

There is an apocryphal story of a physician in the 1940s (a time when no effective medicines for high blood pressure were available) who discovered that restricting the diet of hypertensive patients to plain, boiled, unsalted rice dramatically reduced their blood pressure and also reduced the risk of stroke. The story goes, however, that the diet made the patients so miserable that a lot of them committed suicide.

This is an extreme example, but as recently as last week I have seen guidelines for treating constipation in the elderly that offered no alternative to the combined insults of large amounts of bran and twice daily suppositories. Small wonder that the district nurses who were issued with them (for whom I have a good deal of respect) have gone back to giving castor oil.

For a further discussion on how to incorporate the needs and priorities of patients in guideline development, see a recent report from the College of Health[21].

*Question 9—Did the guidelines include recommendations for their own dissemination, implementation, and regular review?*

Given the well documented gap between what is known to be good practice and what actually happens[11 13 22] and the barriers to the successful implementation of guidelines discussed in section 9.2 it would be in the interests of those who develop guidelines to suggest methods of maximising their use. If this objective were included as standard in the "Guidelines for good guidelines", the guideline writers' output would probably include fewer ivory tower recommendations and more that are plausible, possible, and capable of being explained to patients.

[1] Field MJ, Lohr KN. *Clinical practice guidelines: direction of a new agency.* Washington DC: Institute of Medicine, 1990.

[2] Grimley Evans J. Evidence-based and evidence-biased medicine. *Age Aging* 1995; 24: 461-3.

[3] Edwards P, Jones S, Shale D, *et al. Shared care—a model for clinical management.* Oxford: Radcliffe Medical Press, 1996.

4  Hurwitz B. Clinical guidelines and the law: advice, guidance or regulation? *J Eval Clin Pract* 1995; **1**: 49-60.
5  Chalmers I. Why are opinions about the effects of health care so often wrong? *Medicolegal Journal* 1993; **62**: 116-30.
6  Delamothe T. Wanted: guidelines that doctors will follow. *BMJ* 1993; **307**: 218.
7  Greenhalgh PM. *Shared care for diabetes - a systematic review*. London: Royal College of General Practitioners, 1994. (Occasional Paper 67.)
8  Ayers P, Renvoize T, Robinson M. Clinical guidelines: key decisions for acute service providers. *B J Health Care Management* 1995; **1**: 547-51.
9  Newton J, Knight D, Woolhead G. General practitioners and clinical guidelines: a survey of knowledge, use and beliefs. *B J Gen Pract* 1996; **46**: 513-7.
10 Grimshaw JM, Russell IT. Effect of clinical guidelines on medical practice. A systematic review of rigorous evaluations. *Lancet* 1993; **342**: 1317-22.
11 Lomas J, Haynes RB. A taxonomy and critical review of tested strategies for the application of clinical practice recommendations. From "official" to "individual" clinical policy. *Am J Prev Med* 1987; **4**: 77-94.
12 Royal College of General Practitioners. *The development and implementation of clinical guidelines*. London: Royal College of General Practitioners, 1995. (Report from General Practice 26.)
13 Grimshaw JM, Russell IT. Achieving health gain through guidelines. II. Ensuring guidelines change medical practice. *Quality in Health Care* 1994; **3**: 45-52.
14 Thomson R, Lavender M, Madhok R. How to ensure that guidelines are effective. *BMJ* 1995; **311**: 237-42.
15 Oxman A. *No magic bullets: a systematic review of 102 trials of interventions to help health professionals deliver services more effectively and efficiently*. London: North East Thames Regional Health Authority, 1994.
16 Hayward RSA, Wilson MC, Tunis SR, *et al*. More informative abstracts of articles describing clinical practice guidelines. *Ann Intern Med* 1993; **118**: 731-7.
17 Hayward RSA, Wilson MC, Tunis SR, *et al*. Users' guides to the medical literature. VIII. How to use clinical practice guidelines. A. Are the recommendations valid? *JAMA* 1995; **274**: 570-4.
18 Wilson MC, Hayward RS, Tunis SR, *et al*. Users' guides to the medical literature. VIII. How to use clinical practice guidelines. B. Will the recommendations help me in caring for my patients? *JAMA* 1995; **274**: 1630-2.
19 Nuffield Institute for Health. *Implementing clinical guidelines: can guidelines be used to improve clinical practice?* Leeds: University of Leeds, 1994. (Effective Health Care Bulletin.)
20 Mulrow C. Rationale for systematic reviews. *BMJ* 1994; **309**: 597-9.
21 Kelson M. *Consumer involvement initiatives in clinical audit and outcomes. A review of developments and issues in the identification of good practice*. London: College of Health, 1995.
22 Haines AP. The science of perpetual change. *B J Gen Pract* 1996; **46**: 115-9.

# Chapter 10: Papers that tell you what things cost (economic analyses)

## 10.1 What is economic analysis?

An economic analysis can be defined as *one that entails the use of analytical techniques to define choices in resource allocation*. Most of what I have to say on this subject comes from a short booklet by Professor Michael Drummond[1] and two of the forerunners to the latest "Users' guides to the medical literature"[2][3], all of which emphasise the importance of setting the economic questions about a paper in the context of the overall quality and relevance of the study (see section 10.3).

The first economic evaluation I ever remember was a TV advertisement in which the pop singer Cliff Richard tried to persuade a housewife that the most expensive brand of washing up liquid on the market "actually works out cheaper". It was, apparently, stronger on stains, softer on the hands, and produced more bubbles per penny than "a typical cheap liquid". Although I was only 9 at the time, I was unconvinced. Which "typical cheap liquid" was the product being compared with? How much stronger on stains was it? Why should the effectiveness of a washing up liquid be measured in terms of bubbles produced rather than plates cleaned?

Forgive me for sticking with this trivial example, but I'd like to use it to illustrate the four main types of economic evaluation that you will find in the literature (see table 10.1 for the conventional definitions):

- *Cost-minimisation analysis*—"Sudso" costs 47p per bottle whereas "Jiffo" costs 63p per bottle

- *Cost-effectiveness analysis*—"Sudso" gives you 15 more clean plates per wash than "Jiffo"

- *Cost-utility analysis*—In terms of quality adjusted housewife hours (a composite score reflecting time and effort needed to scrub plates clean and hand roughness caused by the liquid), "Sudso" provides 29 units per pound spent whereas "Jiffo" provides 23 units

- *Cost-benefit analysis*—The net overall cost (reflecting direct cost of the product, indirect cost of time spent washing up, and estimated financial value of a clean plate relative to a slightly grubby one) of "Sudso" per day is 7.17p, while that of "Jiffo" is 9.32p.

Table 10.1 Types of economic analysis

| Type of analysis | Outcome measure | Conditions of use | Example |
|---|---|---|---|
| Cost-minimisation analysis | No outcome measure *= Money saved !* | Used when the effect of both interventions is known (or may be assumed) to be identical | Comparing the price of a brand name drug with that of its generic equivalent when bioequivalence has been demonstrated |
| Cost-effectiveness analysis | Natural units (for example, life years gained) | Used when the effect of the interventions can be expressed in terms of one main variable | Comparing two preventive treatments for an otherwise fatal condition |
| Cost-utility analysis | Utility units (for example, quality adjusted life years) | Used when the effect of the interventions on health status has two or more important dimensions (for example, benefits and side effects of drugs) | Comparing the benefits of two treatments for varicose veins in terms of surgical result, cosmetic appearance, and risk of serious adverse event (for example, pulmonary embolus) |
| Cost-benefit analysis | Monetary units (for example, estimated cost of loss in productivity) | Used when it is desirable to compare an intervention for this condition with an intervention for a different condition | For a purchasing authority, to decide whether to fund a heart transplantation programme or a stroke rehabilitation ward |

*ie. the same units + utility cannot be compared.*

You should be able to see immediately that the most sensible analysis to use in the washing-up liquid example is cost-effectiveness analysis. Cost-minimisation analysis (see table 10.1) is inappropriate as "Sudso" and "Jiffo" do not have identical effectiveness. Cost-utility analysis is unnecessary as, in this example, we are interested in very little else apart from the number of plates cleaned per unit of washing up liquid—in other words, our outcome has only one important dimension. Cost-benefit analysis is, in this example, an absurdly complicated way of telling you that "Sudso" cleans more plates per penny.

There are, however, many settings where health professionals, particularly those who purchase health care from real cash limited budgets, must choose between interventions for a host of different conditions whose outcomes (such as cases of measles prevented, increased mobility after a hip replacement, reduced risk of death from heart attack, or likelihood of giving birth to a live baby) cannot be directly compared with one another. Controversy surrounds not just how these comparisons should be made (see section 10.2) but also who should make them and to whom the decision makers for the "rationing" of health care should be accountable[4] [5]. These essential, fascinating, and frustrating questions are beyond the scope of this book, but if you are interested I would recommend you look up some of the references listed at the end of this chapter.

## 10.2 Measuring the costs and benefits of health interventions

Not long ago, I was taken to hospital to have my appendix removed. From the hospital's point of view, the cost of my care included my board and lodging for five days, a proportion of doctors' and nurses' time, drugs and dressings, and investigations (blood tests and a scan). Other *direct costs* (see box 10.1) included my general practitioner's time for attending me in the middle of the night and the cost of the petrol my husband used when visiting me (not to mention the grapes and flowers).

In addition to this, there were the *indirect* costs of my loss in productivity. I was off work for 3 weeks, and my domestic duties were temporarily divided between various friends, neighbours, and a nice young girl from a nanny agency. And, from my point of view, there were several *intangible* costs, such as discomfort, loss of independence, the allergic rash I developed on the medication, and the cosmetically unsightly scar that I now carry on my abdomen.

---

**Box 10.1 Examples of costs and benefits of health interventions**

| Costs | Benefits |
|---|---|
| *Direct* | *Economic* |
| "Board and lodging" | Prevention of expensive to treat illness |
| Drugs, dressings, etc | Avoidance of hospital admission |
| Investigations | Return to paid work |
| Staff salaries | |
| | |
| *Indirect* | *Clinical* |
| Work days lost | Postponement of death or disability |
| Value of "unpaid" | Relief of pain, nausea, breathlessness, etc |
| work | Improved vision, hearing, muscular strength, etc |
| | |
| *Intangible* | *Quality of life* |
| Pain and suffering | Increased mobility and independence |
| Social stigma | Improved wellbeing |
| | Release from sick role |

---

As box 10.1 shows, these direct, indirect, and intangible costs constitute one side of the cost-benefit equation. On the benefit side, the operation greatly increased my chances of staying alive. In addition, I had a nice rest from work, and, to be honest, I rather enjoyed all the attention and sympathy. (Note that the "social stigma" of appendicitis can be a positive one. I would be less likely to brag about my experience if my hospital admission had been precipitated by, say, an epileptic fit or a nervous breakdown, which have negative social stigmata.)

In the appendicitis example, few patients (and even fewer purchasers) would perceive much freedom of choice in deciding to opt for the operation. But most health interventions do not concern definitive procedures for acutely life threatening diseases. Most of us can count on developing at least one chronic, disabling, and progressive condition such as ischaemic heart disease, high blood pressure, arthritis, chronic bronchitis, cancer, rheumatism, prostatic hypertrophy, or diabetes. At some stage, almost all of us will be forced to decide whether having a routine operation, taking a particular drug, or making a compromise in our lifestyle (reducing our alcohol intake or sticking to a low fat diet) is "worth it".

It is fine for informed individuals to make choices about their own care by gut reaction ("I'd rather live with my hernia than be cut open", or "I know about the risk of thrombosis but I want to continue to smoke and stay on the pill"). But when the choices are about other people's care, subjective judgments are the last thing that should enter the equation. Most of us would want the planners and policymakers to use objective, explicit, and defensible criteria when making decisions such as, "No, Mrs Brown may not have a kidney transplant".

One important way of examining the "what's it worth?" question for a given health state (such as having poorly controlled diabetes or asthma) is to ask someone in that state how they feel. A number of questionnaires have been developed which attempt to measure overall health status, such as the Nottingham health profile, the SF-36 general health questionnaire, and the McMaster health utilities index questionnaire[6].

In some circumstances, disease specific measures of wellbeing are more valid than general measures[7] [8]. For example, answering "yes" to the question, "Do you get very concerned about the food you are eating?" might indicate anxiety in someone without diabetes but normal self care attitudes in someone with diabetes[7]. There has also been an upsurge of interest in *patient specific* measures of quality of life, to allow different patients to place different values on particular aspects of the health and wellbeing[9]. Of course, when quality of life is being analysed from the point of view of the patient, this is a sensible and humane approach. However, the health economist tends to make decisions about groups of patients or populations, in which case patient specific, and even disease specific, measures of quality of life have limited relevance[10].

The authors of standard instruments (such as the SF-36) for measuring the quality of life have often spent years ensuring they are valid (that is, they measure what we think they are measuring), reliable (they do so every time), and responsive to change (that is, if an intervention improves or worsens the patient's health, the scale will reflect that). For this reason, you should be highly suspicious of a paper that eschews these standard instruments in favour of the authors' own rough and ready scale ("functional

142

ability was classified as good, moderate, or poor according to the clinician's overall impression", or "we asked patients to score both their pain and their overall energy level from one to ten and added the results together"). Note also that even instruments that have apparently been well validated often do not stand up to rigorous evaluation of their pyschometric validity[11].

Another way of examining the "what's it worth?" of particular health states is through *health state preference values*—that is, the value that, in a hypothetical situation, a healthy person would place on a particular deterioration in their health or that a sick person would place on a return to health. There are three main methods of assigning such values:

- *Rating scale measurements*—The respondent is asked to make a mark on a fixed line, labelled, for example, "perfect health" at one end and "death" at the other, to indicate where he or she would place the state in question (for example, being wheelchair-bound from arthritis of the hip)

- *Time trade off measurements*—The respondent is asked to consider a particular health state (for example, infertility) and estimate how many of their remaining years in full health they would sacrifice to be "cured" of the condition

- *Standard gamble measurements*—The respondent is asked to consider the choice between living for the rest of their life in a particular health state and taking a "gamble" (for example, an operation) with a given odds of success that would return them to full health if it succeeded but kill them if it failed. The odds are then varied to see at what point the respondent decides the gamble is not worth taking.

The quality adjusted life year or QALY can be calculated by multiplying the preference value for that state with the time the patient is likely to spend in that state. The results of cost-benefit analyses are usually expressed in terms of "cost per QALY", some examples of which are shown in box 10.2[12].

I find it almost impossible to discuss QALYs without my blood starting to boil. Any measure of health state preference values is, at best, a reflection of the preferences and prejudices of the individuals who contributed to its development. Indeed, it is possible to come up with different values for QALYs depending on

143

---

**Box 10.2  Cost per QALY (1990 figures)**

| | |
|---|---:|
| Cholesterol testing and diet therapy | £220 |
| Advice to stop smoking from patient's own doctor | £270 |
| Hip replacement for arthritis | £1180 |
| Kidney transplant | £4710 |
| Breast cancer screening | £5780 |
| Cholesterol testing and drug treatment if indicated (ages 25-39) | £14150 |
| Neurosurgery for malignant brain tumours | £107780 |

---

how the questions from which health state preference values are derived were posed[13].

As medical ethicist John Harris has pointed out, QALYs are, like the society that produces them, inherently ageist, sexist, racist, and loaded against those with permanent disabilities (as even a complete cure of an unrelated condition would not restore the individual to "perfect health"). Furthermore, QALYs distort our ethical instincts by focusing our minds on life years rather than people's lives. A disabled premature infant in need of an intensive care cot will, argues Harris, be allocated more resources than it deserves in comparison with a 50 year old woman with cancer, since the infant, were it to survive, would have so many more life years to quality adjust[14].

Other authors have come up with the HYE or healthy years equivalent, which incorporates the individual's likely improvement or deterioration in health status in the future and is said to avoid some, but not all, of the disadvantages of the QALY[15]. Given that the critics of QALYs and HYEs have offered no alternative all encompassing measure of health status, these utility based units are set to remain in the health economist's toolkit for the forseeable future.

There is, however, another form of analysis that, although it does not abolish the need to place arbitrary numerical values on life and limb, avoids the buck stopping with the unfortunate health economist. This approach, known as *cost consequences analysis,* presents the results of the economic analysis in a disaggregated form. In other words, it expresses different outcomes in terms of their different natural units (that is, something real such as months of survival, legs amputated, or take home babies) so that individuals can assign their own values to particular health states before calculating whether the intervention is "worth it"[1]. Cost-consequences analysis allows for the health state preference values of both individuals and society to change with time and is particularly useful when these are disputed or likely to change. This approach may also allow the analysis to be used by different groups or societies from the ones on which the original trial or survey was performed.

## 10.3 Questions to ask about an economic analysis

The checklist that follows is based on the sources mentioned earlier[1-3] as well as suggestions made by a working party set up by the *British Medical Journal* to produce guidelines for journal editors on appraising economic evaluations (Professor Mike Drummond, personal communication).

*Question 1—Is the analysis based on a study that answers a clearly defined clinical question about an economically important issue?*

Before you attempt to digest what a paper says about costs, quality of life scales, or utilities make sure that the trial being analysed is scientifically relevant and capable of giving unbiased and unambiguous answers to the clinical question posed in its introduction (see chapter 4). Furthermore, if there is clearly little to choose between the interventions in terms of either costs or benefits a detailed economic analysis is probably pointless.

*Question 2—Whose viewpoint are costs and benefits being considered from?*

From the Treasury's point of view the most cost-effective health intervention is one that returns all citizens promptly to taxpayer status and, when this status is no longer tenable, causes immediate sudden death. From the drug company's point of view it would be difficult to imagine a cost-benefit equation that did not contain one of the company's products, and from a physiotherapist's point of view the removal of a physiotherapy service would never be cost-effective. Almost all economic analyses have some funding, and all have been inspired by someone with a vested interest; the paper should say which.

145

*Question 3—Have the interventions being compared been shown to be clinically effective?*

Nobody wants cheap treatment if it doesn't work. The paper you are reading may simply be an economic analysis, in which case it will be based on a previously published clinical trial, or it will be an economic evaluation of a new trial whose clinical results are presented in the same paper. Either way, you must make sure that the intervention that "works out cheaper" is not substantially less effective or more risky in clinical terms than the one that stands to be rejected on the grounds of cost.

*Question 4—Are the interventions sensible and workable in the settings in which they are likely to be applied?*

A research trial that compares one obscure and unaffordable intervention with another will have little impact on medical practice. Remember that standard current practice (which may be "doing nothing") should almost certainly be one of the alternatives compared. Too many research trials look at intervention packages that would be impossible to implement in the non-research setting (they assume, for example, that general practitioners will own a state of the art computer and agree to follow a protocol, that infinite nurse time is available for the taking of blood tests, or that patients will make their personal treatment choices solely on the basis of the trial's conclusions).

*Question 5—Which method of analysis was used and was this appropriate?*

This decision can be summarised as follows (see section 10.2):

- If the interventions produced identical outcomes ⇨ cost-minimisation analysis

- If the important outcome is unidimensional ⇨ cost-effectiveness analysis

- If the important outcome is multidimensional ⇨ cost-utility analysis

- If the cost-benefit equation for this condition needs to be compared with cost-benefit equations for different conditions ⇨ cost-benefit analysis

146

• If a cost-benefit analysis would otherwise be appropriate but the preference values given to different health states are disputed or likely to change ⇨ cost-consequences analysis

*Question 6—How were costs and benefits measured?*

Look back at section 10.2, where I outlined some of the costs associated with my appendix operation. Now imagine a more complicated example—the rehabilitation of stroke patients into their own homes with attendance at a day centre compared with a standard alternative intervention (rehabilitation in a long stay hospital). The economic analysis must take into account not just the time of the various professionals concerned, the time of the secretaries and administrators who help run the service, and the cost of the food and drugs consumed by the stroke patients, but also a fraction of the capital cost of building the day centre and maintaining a transport service to and from it.

There are no hard and fast rules for deciding which costs to include. If you calculate "cost per case" from first principles, remember that someone has to pay for heating, lighting, personnel support, and even the accountants' bills of the institution. In general terms, these "hidden costs" are known as overheads and generally add an additional 30% to 60% on to the cost of a project. The task of costing things like operations and outpatient visits in the UK is easier than it used to be because these experiences are now bought and sold in the internal market at a price that reflects (or should reflect) all overheads involved. Be warned, however, that unit costs of health interventions calculated in one country often bear no relation to those of the same intervention elsewhere, even when these costs are expressed as a proportion of gross national product[16].

Benefits such as earlier return to work for a particular individual can, on the face of it, be measured in terms of the cost of employing that person at his or her usual daily rate. This approach has the unfortunate and politically unacceptable consequence of valuing the health of professional people higher than that of manual workers, homemakers, or the unemployed and that of the white majority higher than that of (generally) lower paid minority ethnic groups[2 3]. It might therefore be preferable to derive the cost of sick days from the average national wage.

In a cost-effectiveness analysis, changes in health status will be expressed in natural units (see section 10.2). But just because the units are natural does not automatically make them appropriate. For example, the economic analysis of the treatment of peptic ulcer by two different drugs might measure outcome as "proportion of ulcers healed after a six week course". Treatments could be compared according to the cost per ulcer healed. If the relapse rates on the two drugs were very different, however, drug A might be falsely deemed "more cost-effective" than drug B. A better outcome measure here might be "ulcers that remained healed at one year".

In cost-benefit analysis, where health status is expressed in utility units such as QALYs, you would, if you were being really rigorous about evaluating the paper, look back at how the particular utilities used in the analysis were derived (see section 10.2). In particular, you will want to know whose health preference values were used—those of patients, doctors, health economists, or the government.

*Question 7—Were incremental, rather than absolute, benefits considered?*

This question is best illustrated by a simple example. Let's say drug X, at £100 per course, cures 10 out of every 20 patients. Its new competitor, drug Y, costs £120 per course and cures 11 out of 20 patients. The cost per case cured with drug X is £200 (since you spent £2000 curing 10 people), and the cost per case cured with drug Y is £218 (since you spent £2400 curing 11 people).

The *incremental* cost of drug Y—that is, the extra cost of curing the extra patient—is *not* £18 but £400, as this is the total amount extra that you have had to pay to achieve an outcome over and above what you would have achieved by giving all patients the cheaper drug. This striking example should be borne in mind the next time a pharmaceutical representative tries to persuade you that his or her product is "more effective and only marginally more expensive".

*Question 8—Was the "here and now" given precedence over the distant future?*

A bird in the hand is worth two in the bush. In health as well as money terms, we value a benefit today more highly than we value a promise of the same benefit in five years' time. When the costs or benefits of an intervention (or lack of the intervention) will occur some time in the future, their value should be *discounted* to reflect this. The actual amount of discount that should be allowed for future as opposed to immediate health benefit is pretty arbitrary, but most analyses use a figure of around 5% a year.

*Question 9—Was a sensitivity analysis performed?*

Let's say a cost-benefit analysis comes out as saying that hernia repair by day case surgery costs £1150 per QALY whereas traditional open repair, with its associated hospital stay, costs £1800 per QALY. But, when you look at how the calculations were done, you are surprised at how cheaply the laparoscopic equipment has been costed. If you raise the price of this equipment by 25%, does day case surgery still come out dramatically cheaper? It may, or it may not.

Sensitivity analysis, or exploration of "what ifs", was described in section 8.2 in relation to meta-analysis. Exactly the same principles apply here: if adjusting the figures to account for the full range of possible influences gives you a totally different answer you should not place too much reliance on the analysis. For a good example of a sensitivity analysis on a topic of both scientific and political importance, see Pharoah and Hollingworth's paper on the cost-effectiveness of lowering cholesterol (which examines the difficult issue of who should receive and who should be denied effective but expensive cholesterol lowering drugs)[17].

*Question 10—Were "bottom line" aggregate scores overused?*

In section 10.2 I introduced the notion of cost-consequences analysis, in which the reader of the paper can attach his or her own values to different utilities. In practice, this is an unusual way of presenting an economic analysis, and, more commonly, the reader is faced with a cost-utility or cost-benefit analysis that gives a composite score in unfamiliar units that do not translate readily into exactly what gains and losses the patient can expect. The situation is analogous to the father who is told, "your child's intelligence quotient is 115" when he would feel far better informed if he were presented with the disaggregated data: "Johnny can read, write, count, and draw pretty well for his age".

## Conclusion

I hope this chapter has shown that the critical appraisal of an economic analysis rests as crucially on asking questions such as,

"Where did those numbers come from?" and "Have any numbers been left out?" as on checking that the sums themselves were correct. While few papers will fulfil all the criteria listed in section 10.3 and summarised in appendix A, you should, after reading the chapter, be able to distinguish an economic analysis of moderate or good methodological quality from one that slips "throwaway costings" into its results or discussion section. For a more in depth discussion of quality of life issues, see the recently published *Users' Guide*[18].

1  Drummond M. *Economic analysis alongside controlled trials.* Leeds: Department of Health, 1994. (Document F51/066 2515 5k. Obtainable from R & D Directorate, NHS Executive, Quarry House, Leeds LS2 7UE.)
2  Drummond MF, Richardson WS, O'Brien BJ, *et al.* Users' guides to the medical literature. XIII. How to use an article on economic analysis of clinical practice. A. Are the results of the study valid? *JAMA* 1997; **277**: 1552-7.
3  O'Brien BJ, Heyland D, Richardson WS, *et al.* Users' guides to the medical literature. XIII. How to use an article on economic analysis of clinical practice. B. What are the results and will they help me in caring for my patients? *JAMA* 1997; **277**: 1802-6.
4  Bowling A. Health care rationing: the public's debate. *BMJ* 1996; **312**: 670-4.
5  Smith R. Rationing health care: moving the debate forward. *BMJ* 1996; **312**:1553-4.
6  Patrick DL, Erikson P. *Health status and health policy.* New York: Oxford University Press, 1993.
7  Bradley C, ed. *Handbook of psychology and diabetes.* London: Harwood Academic Publishers, 1994.
8  Fallowfield LJ. Assessment of quality of life in breast cancer. *Acta Oncol* 1995; **34**: 689-94.
9  Hickey AM, Bury G, O'Boyle CA, *et al.* A new short form individual quality of life measure (SEIQoL-DW). Application in a cohort of individuals with HIV/AIDS. *BMJ* 1996; **313**: 29-33.
10 Cairns J. Measuring health outcomes. *BMJ* 1996; **313**: 6.
11 Gill TM, Feinstein AR. A critical appraisal of the quality of quality of life measurements. *JAMA* 1994; **272**: 619-26.
12 Ham C. Priority setting in the NHS. *Br J Health Care Management* 1995; **1**: 27-9.
13 Weinberger M, Oddone EZ, Samsa G, *et al.* Are health-related quality of life measures affected by the mode of administration? *J Clin Epidemiol* 1996; **49**: 135-40.
14 Harris J. QALYfying the value of life. *J Med Ethics* 1987; **13**: 117-23.
15 Mehrez A, Gafni A. Quality-adjusted life-years, utility theory and healthy years equivalents. *Med Decis Making* 1989; **9**: 142-9.
16 Jefferson T, Demicheli V, Mugford M. *Elementary economic evaluation in health care.* London: BMJ Publishing, 1996.
17 Pharoah PDP, Hollingworth W. Cost-effectiveness of lowering cholesterol concentration with statins in patients with and without pre-existing coronary heart disease: life table method applied to health authority population. *BMJ* 1996; **312**: 1443-8.
18 Guyatt GH, Naylor CD, Juniper E, *et al.* Users' guides to the medical literature. XII. How to use articles about health-related quality of life. *JAMA* 1997; **277**: 1232-7.

# Chapter 11: Papers that go beyond numbers (qualitative research)

## 11.1 What is qualitative research?

The pendulum is swinging. Ten years ago, when I took up my first research post, a work weary colleague advised me: "Find something to measure, and keep on measuring it until you've got a boxful of data. Then stop measuring and start writing up".

"But what should I measure?", I asked.

"That", he said cynically, "doesn't much matter".

This true example illustrates the limitations of an exclusively quantitative (counting and measuring) perspective in research. Epidemiologist Nick Black has argued that a finding or a result is more likely to be accepted as a fact if it is quantified (expressed in numbers) than if it is not[1]. There is little or no scientific evidence, for example, to support the well known "facts" that one couple in 10 is infertile, one man in 10 is homosexual, and half of all cases of diabetes are undiagnosed. Yet, observes Black, most of us are happy to accept uncritically such simplified, reductionist, and blatantly incorrect statements so long as they contain at least one number.

Qualitative researchers seek a deeper truth. They aim to "study things in their natural setting, attempting to make sense of, or interpret, phenomena in terms of the meanings people bring to them"[2], and they use "a holistic perspective which preserves the complexities of human behaviour"[1].

Interpretive or qualitative research was for years the territory of the social scientists. It is now increasingly recognised as being not just complementary to but, in many cases, a prerequisite for the quantitative research with which most of us who trained in the biomedical sciences are more familiar. Certainly, the view that the two approaches are mutually exclusive has itself become "unscientific", and it is currently rather trendy, particularly in the fields of primary care and health services research, to say that you are doing some qualitative research.

Dr Cecil Helman, author of a leading textbook on the anthropological aspects of health and illness[3], told me the following story to illustrate the qualitative-quantitative dichtomy. A small child runs in from the garden and says, excitedly, "Mummy, the leaves are falling off the trees".

"Tell me more", says his mother.

"Well, five leaves fell in the first hour, then 10 leaves fell in the second hour..."

That child will become a quantitative researcher.

A second child, when asked "tell me more", might reply, "Well, the leaves are big and flat, and mostly yellow or red, and they seem to be falling off some trees but not others. And, mummy, why did no leaves fall last month?"

That child will become a qualitative researcher.

Questions such as "How many parents would consult their general practitioner when their child has a mild temperature?" or "What proportion of smokers have tried to give up?" clearly need answering through quantitative methods. But questions like "Why do parents worry so much about their children's temperature?" and "What stops people giving up smoking?" cannot and should not be answered by leaping in and measuring the first aspect of the problem that we (the outsiders) think might be important. Rather, we need to hang out, listen to what people have to say, and explore the ideas and concerns that the subjects themselves come up with. After a while, we may notice a pattern emerging, which may prompt us to make our observations in a different way. We may start with one of the methods shown in box 11.1 and go on to use a selection of others.

---

### Box 11.1 Examples of qualitative research methods

| | |
|---|---|
| Documents | Study of documentary accounts of events, such as meetings |
| Passive observation | Systematic watching of behaviour and talk in naturally occurring settings |
| Participant observation | Observation in which the researcher also occupies a role or part in the setting in addition to observing |
| In depth interviews | Face to face conversation with the purpose of exploring issues or topics in detail. Does not use preset questions but is shaped by a defined set of topics |
| Focus groups | Method of group interview that explicitly includes and uses the group interaction to generate data |

---

Box 11.2, which is reproduced with permission from Nick Mays and Catherine Pope's introductory book *Qualitative Research in Health Care*[4] summarises (indeed overstates) the differences between the qualitative and quantitative approaches to research. In reality, there is a great deal of overlap between them, the importance of which is increasingly being recognised[5].

As section 3.2 explains, quantitative research should begin with an idea (usually articulated as a hypothesis), which then, through measurement, generates data and, by *deduction*, allows a conclusion to be drawn. Qualitative research is different. It begins with an intention to explore a particular area, collects "data" (that is, observations and interviews), and generates ideas and hypotheses from these data largely through what is known as *inductive reasoning*[4]. The strength of the quantitative approach lies in its *reliability* (repeatability)—that is, the same measurements should yield the same results time after time. The strength of qualitative research lies in *validity* (closeness to the truth)—that is, good qualitative research, by using a selection of data collection methods, really should touch the core of what is going on rather

## Box 11.2  Qualitative versus quantitative research—the overstated dichotomy[4]

|  | Qualitative | Quantitative |
|---|---|---|
| Social theory | Action | Structure |
| Methods | Observation, interview | Experiment, survey |
| Question | What is X? (classification) | How many Xs? (enumeration) |
| Reasoning | Inductive | Deductive |
| Sampling method | Theoretical | Statistical |
| Strength | Validity | Reliability |

than just skimming the surface. The validity of qualitative methods is greatly improved by the use of more than one method (see box 11.1) in combination, a process known as *triangulation,* and by more than one researcher analysing the same data independently.

Those who are ignorant about qualitative research often believe that it constitutes little more than hanging out and watching leaves fall. It is beyond the scope of this book to take you through the substantial literature on how to (and how not to) proceed when observing, interviewing, leading a focus group, and so on. But sophisticated methods for all these techniques certainly exist, and if you are interested I suggest you try the introductory[4] or more detailed[2] texts listed at the end of this chapter.

Qualitative methods really come into their own in the research of uncharted territory—that is, where the variables of greatest concern are poorly understood, ill defined, and cannot be controlled[1 6]. In such circumstances, the definitive hypothesis may not be arrived at until the study is well underway. But it is in precisely these circumstances that the qualitative researcher must ensure that she or he has, at the outset, carefully delineated a particular focus of research and identified some specific questions to try to answer (see question 1 in section 11.2 below). The methods of qualitative research allow for, and even encourage[2], modification of the research question in the light of findings generated along the way. (In contrast, sneaking a look at the interim results of a quantitative study is statistically invalid! (p 75.))

The so-called *iterative* approach (altering the research methods and the hypothesis as you go along) employed by qualitative researchers shows a commendable sensitivity to the richness and variability of the subject matter. Failure to recognise the legitimacy of this approach has, in the past, led critics to accuse qualitative researchers of continually moving their own goalposts. While these criticisms are often misguided, there is, as Nicky Britten and colleagues have observed, a real danger "that the flexibility [of the iterative approach] will slide into sloppiness as the researcher ceases to be clear about what it is (s)he is investigating"[6]. They warn that qualitative researchers must, therefore, allow periods away from their fieldwork for reflection, planning, and consultation with colleagues.

## 11.2 Evaluating papers that describe qualitative research

By its very nature, qualitative research is non-standard, unconfined, and dependent on the subjective experience of both the researcher and the researched. It explores what needs to be explored and cuts its cloth accordingly. It is debatable, therefore, whether an all encompassing critical appraisal checklist along the lines of the "Users' guides to the medical literature" (see references 8–19 in chapter 3) could ever be developed. My own view and that of several people who have also enquired, or are currently working on this very task[4 6] is that such a checklist may not be as exhaustive or as universally applicable as the various guides for appraising quantitative research, but that it is certainly possible to set some ground rules. The list that follows has been distilled from the published work cited earlier[2 4 6] and also from discussions with Dr Rod Taylor of Exeter University, who is currently piloting a more detailed and extensive critical appraisal guide for qualitative papers.

*Question 1—Did the paper describe an important clinical problem examined through a clearly formulated question?*

In section 3.2, I explained that one of the first things you should look for in any research paper is a statement of why the research was done and what specific question it examined. Qualitative papers are no exception to this rule: there is absolutely no scientific value in interviewing or observing people just for the sake of it. Papers that cannot define their topic of research more closely than "we decided to interview 20 patients with epilepsy" inspire little confidence that the researchers really knew what they were studying or why.

You might be more inclined to read on if the paper stated in its introduction something like, "Epilepsy is a common and potentially disabling condition, and up to 20% of patients do not remain free of fits on medication. Antiepileptic medication is known to have unpleasant side effects, and several studies have shown that a high proportion of patients do not take their tablets regularly. We therefore decided to explore patients' beliefs about epilepsy and their perceived reasons for not taking their medication".

As I explained in section 11.1, the iterative nature of qualitative research is such that the definitive research question may not be clearly focused at the outset of the study, but as Britten and colleagues point out, it should certainly have been formulated by the time the report is written.[6]

*Question 2—Was a qualitative approach appropriate?*

If the objective of the research was to explore, interpret, or obtain a deeper understanding of a particular clinical issue, qualitative methods were almost certainly the most appropriate ones to use. If, however, the research aimed to achieve some other goal (such as determining the incidence of a disease or the prevalence of an adverse drug reaction, testing a cause and effect hypothesis, or showing that one drug has a better risk-benefit ratio than another) qualitative methods are clearly inappropriate! If you think a case-control, cohort study, or randomised trial would have been better suited to the research question posed in the paper than the qualitative methods that were actually used, you might like to compare that question with the examples in sections 3.3 to 3.7 to confirm your hunch.

*Question 3—How were the setting and the subjects selected?*

Look back at box 11.2, which contrasts the *statistical* sampling methods of quantitative research with *theoretical* ones of qualitative research. Let me explain what this means. In the earlier chapters of this book, particularly section 4.2, I emphasised the importance in quantitative research of ensuring that a truly random sample of subjects is recruited. A random sample will ensure that the results reflect, *on average*, the condition of the population from which that sample was drawn.

In qualitative research, however, we are not interested in an "on average" view of a patient population. We want to gain an in depth understanding of the experience of particular individuals or groups, and we should, therefore, deliberately seek out individuals or groups who fit the bill. If, for example, we wanted to study the experience of non-English speaking British Punjabi women when they gave birth in hospital (with a view to tailoring the interpreter/advocacy service more closely to the needs of this patient group) we would be perfectly justified in going out of our way to find women who had had a range of different birth experiences—an induced delivery, an emergency caesarean section, a delivery by a medical student, a late miscarriage, and so on.

We would also want to select some women who had had shared antenatal care between an obstetrician and their general practitioner and some women who had been cared for by community midwives throughout the pregnancy. In this example, it might be particularly instructive to find women who had had their care provided by male doctors, even though this would be a relatively unusual situation. Finally, we might choose to study patients who gave birth in the setting of a large, modern, "high tech" maternity unit as well as some who did so in a small community hospital. Of course, all these specifications will give us "biased" samples, but that is exactly what we want.

Watch out for qualitative research in which the sample has been selected (or seems to have been selected) purely on the basis of convenience. In the above example, taking the first dozen Punjabi patients to pass through the nearest labour ward would be the easiest way to notch up interviews, but the information obtained may be considerably less helpful.

*Question 4 What was the researcher's perspective and has this been taken into account?*

Given that qualitative research is necessarily grounded in real life experience a paper describing such research should not be "trashed" simply because the researchers have declared a

157

particular cultural perspective or personal involvement with the subjects of the research. Quite the reverse; they should be congratulated for doing just that. It is important to recognise that there is no way of abolishing or fully controlling for observer bias in qualitative research. This is most obviously the case when participant observation (see box 11.1) is used, but it is also true for other forms of data collection and of data analysis.

If, for example, the research concerns the experience of asthmatic adults living in damp and overcrowded housing and the perceived effect of these surroundings on their health, the data generated by techniques such as focus groups or semistructured interviews are likely to be heavily influenced by what the *interviewer* believes about this subject and by whether he or she is employed by the hospital chest clinic, the social work department of the local authority, or an environmental pressure group. But as it is inconceivable that the interviews could have been conducted by someone with no views at all and no ideological or cultural perspective, the most that can be required of the researchers is that they describe in detail  where they are coming from so that the results can be interpreted accordingly.

*Question 5—What methods did the researcher use for collecting data and are these described in enough detail?*

I once spent two years doing highly quantitative, laboratory based experimental research in which around 15 hours of every week were spent filling or emptying test tubes. There was a standard way to fill the test tubes, a standard way to spin them in the centrifuge, and even a standard way to wash them up. When I finally published my research, some nine hundred hours of drudgery was summed up in a single sentence: "Patients' serum rhubarb levels were measured according to the method described by Bloggs and Bloggs [reference to Bloggs and Bloggs' paper on how to measure serum rhubarb]".

I now spend quite a lot of my time doing qualitative research, and I can confirm that it's infinitely more fun. I and my research assistant have spent the last year devising a unique combination of techniques to measure the beliefs, hopes, fears and attitudes of diabetic patients from a particular minority ethnic group (British Bangladeshis). We have had to develop, for example, a valid way of simultaneously translating and transcribing interviews that were conducted in Sylheti, a complex dialect of Bengali that has no

158

written form. We have found that patients' attitudes seem to be heavily influenced by the presence in the room of certain of their relatives, so we have contrived to interview some patients in both the presence and the absence of these key relatives.

I could go on describing the methods we devised to examine this particular research issue, but I have probably made my point: the methods section of a qualitative paper often cannot be written in shorthand or dismissed by reference to someone else's research techniques. It may have to be lengthy and discursive as it is telling a unique story without which the results cannot be interpreted. As with the sampling strategy, there are no hard and fast rules about exactly what details should be included in this section of the paper. You should simply ask, "Have I been given enough information about the methods used?", and, if you have, use your common sense to assess, "Are these methods a sensible and adequate way of examining the research question?"

*Question 6—What methods did the researcher use to analyse the data and what quality control measures were implemented?*

The data analysis section of a qualitative research paper is where sense can most readily be distinguished from nonsense. Having amassed a thick pile of completed interview transcripts or field notes, the genuine qualitative researcher has hardly begun. It is simply not good enough to flick through the text looking for "interesting quotes" that support a particular theory. The researcher must find a *systematic* way of analysing his or her data and, in particular, must seek examples of cases that seem to contradict or challenge the theories derived from the majority.

One way of doing this is via *content analysis:* drawing up a list of coded categories and "cutting and pasting" each segment of transcribed data into one of these categories. This can be done either manually or, if large amounts of data are to be analysed, via a tailor made computer database. The statements made by all the subjects on a particular topic can then be compared with one another, and more sophisticated comparisons can be made such as "Did people who made statement A also tend to make statement B?"

A good qualitative research paper will show evidence of "quality control"—that is, the data (or at least, a sample of them) will have been analysed by more than one researcher to confirm that they are both assigning the same meaning to them. In analysing my own research into health beliefs in diabetic patients, three of us are looking in turn at a typed interview transcript and assigning codings to particular statements. Our analysis will almost certainly reveal differences in the interpretation we assign to certain statements. We will try to resolve these disagreements by discussion and when this fails we may ask a fourth party to have the casting vote. All this is legitimate methodology for analysing qualitative data. What is *not* legitimate is to assume that one person's interpretation of the data can be set in stone, however experienced or clever they are! Nevertheless, there is a good deal of debate amongst qualitative researchers about how quality control can or should be undertaken in this type of research.

*Question 7—Are the results credible, and if so, are they important in practice?*

We obviously cannot assess the credibility of qualitative results through the precision and accuracy of measuring devices nor their significance through confidence intervals and numbers needed to treat. It often takes little more than plain common sense to determine whether the results of a qualitative study are sensible and believable and whether they matter in practice.

One important aspect of the results section to check is whether the authors cite actual data. Claims such as "general practitioners did not usually recognise the value of audit" would be infinitely more credible if one or two verbatim quotes from the interviewees were reproduced to illustrate them. The results should be independently and objectively verifiable—after all, a subject either made a particular statement or not—and all quotes and examples should be indexed so that they can be traced back to an indentifiable subject and setting.

*Question 8—What conclusions were drawn and are they justified by the results?*

A quantitative research paper, presented in standard IMRAD format (see section 3.1) should clearly distinguish the study's results (usually a set of numbers) from the interpretation of those results. The reader should have no difficulty separating what the researchers *found* from what they think it *means*. In qualitative research, however, such a distinction is rarely possible as the results are by definition an interpretation of the data.

160

It is therefore necessary when you assess the validity of qualitative research to ask whether the interpretation placed on the data accords with common sense and is relatively untainted with personal or cultural prejudice. This can be a difficult exercise because the language we use to describe things tends to impugn meanings and motives that the subjects themselves may not share. Compare, for example, the two statements, "three women went to the well to get water" and "three women met at the well and each was carrying a pitcher".

It is becoming a cliché that the conclusions of qualitative studies, like those of all research, should be "grounded in evidence"—that is, that they should flow from what the researchers found in the field. Mays and Pope suggest three useful questions for determining whether the conclusions of a qualitative study are valid:

- How well does this analysis explain why people behave in the way they do?

- How comprehensive would this explanation be to a thoughtful participant in the setting?

- How well does the explanation cohere with what we already know?[7]

*Question 9—Are the findings of the study transferable to other clinical settings?*

One of the commonest criticisms of qualitative research is that the findings of any qualitative study pertain only to the limited setting in which they were obtained. In fact, this is not necessarily any truer of qualitative research than of quantitative research. Look back at the example of British Punjabi women I described in question 3. You should be able to see that the use of a true *theoretical* sampling frame greatly increases the transferability of the results over a "convenience" sample.

## Conclusion

Doctors have traditionally placed high value on number based data, which may in reality be misleading, reductionist, and irrelevant to the real issues. The increasing popularity of qualitative research in the biomedical sciences has risen largely because quantitative methods provided either no answers or the wrong answers to important questions in both clinical care and service delivery[1]. If you still feel that qualitative research is necessarily second rate by virtue of being a "soft" science, you should be aware that you are out of step with the evidence[8].

In 1993, Catherine Pope and Nicky Britten presented at a conference a paper entitled "Barriers to qualitative methods in the medical mindset", in which they showed their collection of rejection letters from biomedical journals[9]. The letters revealed a striking ignorance of qualitative methodology on the part of reviewers. In other words, the people who had rejected the papers often seemed to be incapable of distinguishing good qualitative research from bad.

Somewhat ironically, poor quality qualitative papers now appear regularly in some medical journals, who seem to have undergone an about face in editorial policy since Pope and Britten's exposure of the "medical mindset". I hope, therefore, that the questions listed above and the references below will assist reviewers in both camps: those who continue to reject qualitative papers for the wrong reasons and those who have climbed on the qualitative bandwagon and are now *accepting* such papers for the wrong reasons! Note, however, that the critical appraisal of qualitative research is a relatively underdeveloped science and the questions posed in this chapter are still being refined.

[1] Black N. Why we need qualitative research. *J Epidemiol Community Health* 1994; **48**: 425-6.

[2] Denzin NK, Lincoln YS, eds. *Handbook of qualitative research.* London: Sage Publications, 1994.

[3] Helman C. *Culture, health and illness.* 3rd ed. London: Butterworth Heinemann, 1995.

[4] Mays N, Pope C, eds. *Qualitative research in health care.* London: BMJ Publishing, 1996.

[5] Abell P. Methodological achievements in sociology over the past few decades with specific reference to the interplay of qualitative and quantitative methods. In: Bryant C, Becker H, eds. *What has sociology achieved?* London: Macmillan Publishing, 1990.

[6] Britten N, Jones R, Murphy E, *et al.* Qualitative research methods in general practice and primary care. *Fam Prac* 1995; **12**: 104-14.

[7] Mays N, Pope C, eds. *Qualitative research in health care.* London: BMJ Publishing, 1996: 15.

[8] Kinmonth A-L. Understanding and meaning in research and practice. *Fam Pract* 1995; **12**: 1-2.

[9] Pope C, Britten N. *The quality of rejection: barriers to qualitative methods in the medical mindset. Paper presented at BSA Medical Sociology Group annual conference, September 1993.*

# Chapter 12:
# Implementing evidence based findings

## 12.1 Surfactants *v* steroids: a case study in adopting evidence based practice

I recently overheard a new minor surgery nurse being shown the ropes in our general practice by one who had been working there for some years. "Dr A likes the instruments sterilised for 20 minutes; all the others want 10; Dr C will never use nylon sutures; Dr E insists on applying antibiotic spray to all surgical wounds...".

And so it went on, underlining the painful truth that our operating styles were so idiosyncratic that the nurses had resorted to keeping a written checklist of our preferences. We all, no doubt, believe ourselves to have very good reasons for practising the way we do, and, as our staff will testify, we are all stubbornly resistant to change.

Doctors' failure to practice in accordance with the best available evidence cannot, however, be attributed entirely to cussedness. Consultant paediatrician Dr Vivienne Van Someren described an example to me that illustrates many of the additional barriers to getting research evidence into practice: the prevention of neonatal respiratory distress syndrome in premature babies.

It was discovered back in 1957 that babies born more than 6 weeks early may get into severe breathing difficulties because of lack of a substance called surfactant (which lowers the surface tension within the lung alveoli and reduces resistance to expansion) in their lungs. Pharmaceutical companies began research in the 1960s to develop an artificial surfactant that could be given to the infant to prevent the life threatening syndrome developing, but it was not until the mid-1980s that an effective product was developed.

By the late 1980s a number of randomised trials had taken place, and a meta-analysis published in 1990 suggested that the benefits of artificial surfactant greatly outweighed its risks. In 1990, a 6000 patient trial (OSIRIS) was begun that involved almost all the major neonatal intensive care units in the UK. The manufacturer was awarded a product licence in 1990, and by 1993, practically every eligible premature infant in the UK was receiving artificial surfactant.

Another treatment had also been shown a generation ago to prevent the neonatal respiratory distress syndrome: administration of the steroid drug dexamethasone to mothers in premature labour. Dexamethasone worked by accelerating the rate at which the fetal lung reached maturity. Its efficacy had been demonstrated in experimental animals in 1969 and in clinical trials on humans published in the prestigious journal *Paediatrics* as early as 1972. Yet despite a significant beneficial effect being confirmed in a number of further trials and a meta-analysis published in 1990, the take up of this technology was astonishingly slow. It was estimated in 1995 that only 12%-18% of eligible mothers currently received this treatment in the United States[1].

The quality of the evidence and the magnitude of the effect were similar for both these treatments[2][3]. Why were the paediatricians so much quicker than the obstetricians at implementing an intervention that prevented avoidable deaths? Dr Van Someren has considered several factors, listed in table 12.1. The effect of artificial surfactant is virtually immediate, and the doctor administering it witnesses directly the "cure" of a terminally sick baby. Pharmaceutical industry support for a large (and, arguably, scientifically unnecessary) trial ensured that few consultant paediatricians appointed in the early 1990s would have escaped being introduced to the new technology.

In contrast, steroids, particularly for pregnant women, were unfashionable and perceived by patients to be "bad for you". In doctors' eyes, dexamethasone treatment was old hat for a host of unglamorous diseases, notably cancer, and the scientific mechanism for its effect on fetal lungs was not readily understood. Most poignantly of all, an obstetrician would rarely get a chance to witness directly the life saving effect on an individual patient.

Table 12.1  Factors influencing implementation of evidence to prevent neonatal respiratory distress syndrome (Dr V Van Someren, personal communication)

| Factor | Surfactant treatment | Surfactant steroid treatment |
|---|---|---|
| Perception of mechanism | Corrects a surfactant deficiency disease | Ill defined effect on developing lung tissue |
| Timing of effect | Minutes | Days |
| Impact on prescriber | Views effect directly (has to stand by ventilator) | Sees effect as statistic in annual report |
| Perception of side effects | Perceived as minimal | Clinicians' and patients' anxiety disproportionate to actual risk |
| Conflict between two patients | No (paediatrician's patient will benefit directly) | Yes (obstetrician's patient will not benefit directly) |
| Pharmaceutical industry interest | High (patented product; huge potential revenue) | Low (product out of patent; small potential revenue) |
| Trial technology | "New" (developed in late 1980s) | "Old" (developed in early 1970s) |
| Widespread involvement of clinicians in trials | Yes | No |

The above example is far from isolated. Effective health care strategies often take years to catch on[1], even among the experts who should be at the cutting edge of practice[5]. It would seem that for a new technology to be adopted readily by individual health professionals several conditions must be satisfied. The evidence should be unequivocal and of high quality (preferably from large randomised controlled trials with well defined, clinically important end points); the user of the technology must personally believe that it is effective; he or she should have the opportunity to try out the intervention in controlled circumstances; possible adverse effects of the technology should be placed in proportion to the likely benefits; and clinical conflicts of interest (for example, an obstetrician's divided loyalty between two patients) should be identified and explored.

## 12.2 Changing the behaviour of health professionals

A review by Greco and Eisenberg in the *New England Journal of Medicine* summarises various methods that have been evaluated for changing physicians' behaviour[6]. These include feedback, strategies that encourage "ownership" of the changes, administrative rules, financial incentives, financial penalties, and educational interventions. Andy Haines, in the *British Journal of General Practice*, considers a number of others, particularly social influence strategies, computerised decision support systems, and informed consumers[7]. All these are considered in turn below.

*Feedback* consists of telling the clinician how his or her performance (for example, number of hysterectomies performed per head of population, total cost of drugs prescribed per month, and so on) over time compares either with a group norm (such as the levels achieved by fellow clinicians) or with an external standard (such as expert consensus). Studies have given apparently conflicting results on the effectiveness of feedback[6] and suggest that it is effective in changing practice only if the health professional already accepts that his or her practice needs to change; he or she has the resources and authority to implement the required changes; and the feedback is offered in "real time" (that is, at the time when the practice is being implemented) rather than retrospectively[6].

The importance of *ownership* (that is, the feeling by those being asked to play by new rules that they have been involved in drawing up those rules) was emphasised in section 9.2 in relation to clinical guidelines[8]. There is an extensive management theory literature to support the common sense notion that professionals will oppose changes that they perceive as threatening to their livelihood (i.e., income), self esteem, sense of competence, or autonomy[9]. It stands to reason, therefore, that involving health professionals in setting the standards against which they are going to be judged generally produces greater changes in patient outcomes than occur if they are not involved[10].

*Administrative* strategies for influencing clinicians' behaviour include, at one extreme, changes in the law (for example, withdrawing the product licence for a drug) or institutional policy (such as the imposition of a restricted formulary of drugs and equipment). More commonly, they involve introducing barriers to undesired practice (such as requiring the approval of a specialist when ordering certain tests) or reducing barriers to desired practice (such as altering order forms to reflect the preferred dosing interval for antibiotics)[11]. *Financial incentives* may be set up to prompt health professionals to perform more of a desired intervention (such as the UK "target" system for cervical smears by general practitioners[12]) or less of an undesired one (such as changing a fee for service remuneration policy for clinic doctors to a flat rate salary[13]).

Such strategies, however, may run counter to the philosophy of involving professionals in setting standards and gaining their ownership of the changes. In addition, while the evidence that administrative and financial strategies achieve changes in behaviour is strong, these changes may generate much resented "hassle" and are not always translated into desired patient outcomes[6]. A restrictive policy to minimise "unnecessary" drug prescribing in the elderly, for example, achieved its limited objective of reducing expenditure on medication but was associated with increased rates of admission to nursing homes[14]. This illustrates the important point that implementing evidence based practice is not an all or none, unidimensional achievement, as I have argued elsewhere[15].

Until relatively recently *education* (at least in relation to the training of doctors) was more or less synonymous with the didactic talk and chalk sessions that most of us remember from school and college. Such lecture based education is relatively cheap and convenient for the educators but is largely ineffective in producing sustained behaviour change in practice[16]. Education that is hands on and structured around real clinical problems identified by doctors, nurses or students ("problem based learning") is far more effective[17] and has been applied successfully to practising clinicians in the UK[18]. Unfortunately, however, education by problem based learning is still considered to be impractical or unaffordable by many undergraduate and postgraduate educational institutions, notably many medical and nursing schools, in the UK[19].

One method of "education" that the pharmaceutical industry has shown to be highly effective is one to one contact between doctors and company representatives (known in the United States as detailers), whose influence on clinical behaviour may be so dramatic that they have been dubbed the "stealth bombers" of medicine[20]. In the United States this tactic has been harnessed by the government in what is known as *academic detailing:* the educator books in to see the physician in the same way as industry representatives, but in this case the "rep" provides objective, complete, and comparative information about a range of different drugs and encourages the clinician to adopt a critical approach to the evidence. Such a strategy can achieve dramatic short term changes in practice[21] but may be ineffective if the educator attends only briefly and fails to ascertain the perspective of the clinician before attempting to influence it[22].

Academic detailing is one example of a general behaviour change policy known as *social influence,* in which the practitioner is persuaded that his or her current practice is out of step with that of colleagues or experts[23]. Social influence policies also include use of the mass media, processes in which members of a group or network influence one another[24], and those in which local opinion leaders are used as a mouthpiece for policy change[25]. A systematic review by Andy Oxman and colleagues provides some overall support for these methods but gives several examples of so called social influence policies that, in reality, failed to influence[26].

There is a growing literature on the use of high technology strategies such as computerised *decision support systems* that incorporate the best research evidence and can be accessed by the busy practitioner at the touch of a button. Dozens of these systems are currently being developed, and within a few years their effect on both clinicians' practice and patient outcomes will probably be well documented. Currently, however, there is little reliable evidence on their efficacy in practice: a recent systematic review found that of 28 studies identified that set out to evaluate computerised decision support systems, only seven were of high quality[27].

One important method of initiating change in the behaviour of health professionals is *pressure from patients and the general public.* A number of organisations now produce evidence based information leaflets for patients—for example, the "Effectiveness matters" series based on the *Effective Health Care Bulletin* from the Centre for Reviews and Dissemination in York[28], the MIDIRS booklet *Through the Maze*[29], which is based, among other sources, on the Cochrane Pregnancy and Childbirth Database, or the British Diabetic Association's leaflet *Diabetes care: what you should expect*[30]. A number of electronic information aids on particular conditions are now available either as interactive video discs[31] or over the Internet[32].

The power of informed patient choice can also be harnessed more directively—for example, through the "prompted care" model of diabetes care, where patients are sent a structured checklist of tasks (such as blood pressure monitoring and inspection of feet) every six months and advised to ask their doctor to complete it[33]. For an overview of the patient's perspective in evidence based health care and examples of how the informed user can shape the behaviour of professionals, see Fulford, Ersser, and Hope's new book, *Essential Practice in Patient-centred Care*[34].

In summary, there is no shortage of strategies for changing the behaviour of health professionals, but at the time of writing, few have been rigorously evaluated. As Oxman and colleagues concluded after reviewing 102 published studies on different ways to influence the behaviour of clinicians, "there are no 'magic bullets' for improving the quality of health care, but there is a wide range of interventions available that, if used appropriately, could lead to important improvements in professional practice and patient outcomes"[26].

## 12.3 Introducing change in organisations

Large organisations such as hospitals or health authorities usually operate in a bureaucracy culture, where tradition dies hard and practical barriers to change may be considerable. Private industry has led the field in developing management mechanisms to introduce innovations in such organisations[35], but, by and large, the public health care sector does not possess these mechanisms[i]. There is growing interest, however, in the adaptation of the principles of total quality management[35] (known in the context of health care as continuous quality improvement or CQI) to the improvement of health care and the systems for delivering it. In principle, CQI applied to health care involves the following steps[36].

- Convene a multidisciplinary team of health care practitioners and support staff

- Identify the problem through careful study of relevant organisational systems and processes and by collection and analysis of data

- Identify or develop appropriate clinical practice guidelines to solve the problem

- Consider barriers to the implementation of these guidelines

- Develop strategies to deal with the barriers

- Implement the guidelines and associated strategies

- Measure performance

- Review the results

- Repeat the process as necessary

In other words, the CQI approach entails fostering an evaluative culture within the organisation, identifying the health care equivalent of the "customer supply chain(s)", and empowering relevant individuals to make changes at the grass roots. Representative participation in the CQI process from all professional and ancillary groups within the organisation should achieve at least some degree of ownership of the final strategy by everyone involved in implementing it. It should, in addition, allow the dissemination of the required changes to occur from within these ranks rather than being imposed from outside[23]. The evaluation of CQI initiatives within the public health care sector has only recently begun, but the results of several ongoing studies (in one of which I am involved) are keenly awaited.

One project that has looked systematically at the implementation of evidence based findings in health care organisations is the GRiPP (Getting Research into Practice and Purchasing) initiative of the Anglia and Oxford Regional Health Authority in the UK[37]. This project was founded on the view that it was not sensible to rely on one course of action—such as producing a set of clinical guidelines—but rather that the overall process had to be managed by using all the ways and means available. A number of separate projects were initiated through GRiPP, including the use of steroids in preterm delivery, the management of services for stroke patients, the use of dilatation and curettage in women with heavy periods, and insertion of grommets into children with glue ear. The lessons in box 12.1 were the result of a rigorous evaluation process undertaken by the different participating groups[38].

---

**Box 12.1  Lessons from the GRiPP (Getting Research into Practice and Purchasing) project[38]**

- Prerequisites for implementing changes in clinical practice are *nationally available research evidence* and *clear, robust, and local justification for change*
- There should be *consultation and involvement* of all interested parties, led by a respected product champion
- The *knock on* effect of change in one sector (for example, acute services) on to others (for example, general practice or community care) should be examined
- *Information* about current practice and the effect of change needs to be available
- *Relationships* between purchasers and providers need to be good
- Contracts (for example, between purchasers and providers) are best used to *summarise agreement* that has already been negotiated elsewhere, not to table points for discussion
- Implementing evidence *may not save money*
- Implementing evidence *takes more time than is usually anticipated*

---

## 12.4  Implementing evidence based practice in health authorities and trusts

A publication by the UK National Association of Health Authorities and Trusts (NAHAT) entitled *Acting on the Evidence* observes that "however hard the organisations responsible for producing... effectiveness information try, they cannot change practice themselves. Only health authorities and trusts, and the managers and clinicians who work within them, have the power (and the responsibility) to translate the evidence into real, meaningful and lasting improvements in patient care"[38]. The report recognises that the task of educating and empowering managers and clinical professionals to use evidence as part of their everyday decision making is massive and offers advice for any organisation wishing to promote the principles of evidence based practice. An action checklist for health care organisations working towards an evidence based culture for clinical and purchasing decisions, summarised at the end of appendix A, may be found in full in the NAHAT report[38].

First and foremost, key players within the organisation, particularly chief executives, board members, and senior clinicians, must create an evidence based culture in which decision making is

171

*expected* to be based on the best available evidence. High quality, up to date information sources (such as the Cochrane electronic library and the Medline database) should be available in every office and staff given protected time to access them. Ideally, users should have to deal with only a single access point for all available sources. Information on the clinical and cost effectiveness of particular technologies should be produced, disseminated, and used together. Individuals who collate and disseminate this information within the organisation need to be aware of who will use it and how it will be applied—and tailor their presentation accordingly. They should also set standards for and evaluate the quality of the evidence they are distributing.

Individuals on the organisation's internal mailing list for effectiveness information need training and support if they are to make the best use of this information. The GRiPP project provided important practical lessons (see box 12.1), but there is much still to learn about the practicalities of implementing evidence within large (and small) organisations. As the NAHAT report emphasises, separately funded pilot projects on specific clinical issues such as GRiPP[37] are useful for demonstrating that change is possible and offering on the job training in implementing evidence, but health authorities and trusts must now move on from this experimental phase and work towards a culture in which clinical and cost effectiveness are part of the routine dialogue between purchasers and providers and between managers and clinicians.

## 12.5 Priorities for further research on the implementation process

Following the success of GRiPP, the UK Department of Health has identified further studies into the implementation of evidence based policy as a major spoke of its research and development strategy[39] and made training in research methodology a statutory requirement for all doctors undergoing higher professional training[40]. The 20 priority areas in which new research proposals were specifically invited by the NHS Central Research and Development Committee include the following questions[41]:

- Who are the players in the implementation process? Research is needed to examine the relative roles of individuals, professionals, purchasers, providers, the public, the media, commercial organisations, and policymakers in the implementation process.

● What are the levers of change and barriers to change? Research could investigate the effectiveness in achieving change of contracts (as used in the UK internal market), financial incentives, professional and regulatory pressures, organisational incentives and disincentives, and structural issues.

● What interventions can be used to bring about change? A range of interventions could be explored, including the use of guidelines, clinical audit, feedback, outreach visits, consensus building processes, opinion leaders, patient pressures, process redesign, and decision support or reminder systems.

● How does the nature of the evidence affect the implementation process? Additional studies are required into the nature of the evidence underlying current and proposed clinical practices, the availability, strength, and relevance of evidence from randomised controlled trials; the use of observational information, qualitative data, and other evidence from non-randomised controlled trials; the integration of evidence from disparate sources, and the transfer of evidence from one setting to another.

1 Anonymous. Effect of corticosteroids for fetal maturation on perinatal outcomes. NIH consensus development panel on the effect of corticosteroids for fetal maturation on perinatal outcomes. *JAMA* 1995; **273**: 413-8.
2 Crowley P. *Corticosteroids prior to preterm delivery (updated January 1996). Cochrane Database of Systematic Reviews.* London: BMJ Publishing, 1996.
3 Halliday HL. Overview of clinical trials comparing natural and synthetic surfactants. Biology of the Neonate 1995; **67** (suppl 1): 32-47.
4 Haines A, Jones R. Implementing findings of research. *BMJ* 1994; **308**: 1488-92.
5 Antmann EM, Lau J, Kupelnick B, *et al.* A comparison of the results of meta-analyses of randomised controlled trials and recommendations of clinical experts. *JAMA* 1992; **268**: 240-8.
6 Greco PJ, Eisenberg JM. Changing physicians' behavior. *N Engl J Med* 1993; **329**: 1271-4.
7 Haines AP. The science of perpetual change. *B J Gen Pract* 1996; **46**: 115-9.
8 Grimshaw JM, Russell IT. Effect of clinical guidelines on medical practice. A systematic review of rigorous evaluations. *Lancet* 1993; **342**: 1317-22.
9 Laffel G. Blumenthal D. The case for using industrial quality management science in health care organizations. *JAMA* 1989; **262**:2869-73.

[10] Royal College of General Practitioners. *The development and implementation of clinical guidelines.* London: Royal College of General Practitioners, 1995. (Report from General Practice 26.)

[11] Avorn J, Soumerai SB, Taylor W, *et al.* Reduction of incorrect antibiotic dosing through a structured educational order form. *Arch Intern Med* 1988; **148:** 1720-4.

[12] Ridsdale L. Screening for carcinoma of the cervix. In: *Evidence-based general practice: a critical reader.* London: WB Saunders, 1995; 59-76.

[13] Hickson GB, Altemeier WA, Perrin JM. Physician reimbursement by salary or fee-for-service: effect on physician practice behavior in a randomised prospective trial. *Pediatrics* 1987; **80:** 344-50.

[14] Soumerai SB, Ross-Degnan D, Avorn J, *et al.* Effects of Medicaid drug-payment limits on admission to hospitals and nursing homes. *N Engl J Med* 1991; **325:** 1072-7.

[15] Greenhalgh T. Is my practice evidence based? (editorial). *BMJ* 1996; **313:** 957-8.

[16] Davis DA, Thomson MA, Oxman AD. Changing physician performance: a systematic review of the effect of CME strategies. *JAMA* 1995; **274:** 700-5.

[17] Vernon DT, Blake RL. Does problem-based learning work: a meta-analysis of evaluative research. *Acad Med* 1993; **68:**550-63.

[18] Steigler ST, Fatok-Yttery, Hupe K. General practice continuing education— initial experiences with problem-based learning in a continuing education program. *Zeitschrift fur Arztliche Fortbildung* 1995; **89:** 355-8.

[19] Greenhalgh T. Educational courses in evidence-based medicine. *Evidence-Based Medicine* 1997; **2:** 7-8.

[20] Shaughnessy AF, Slawson DC. Pharmaceutical representatives. *BMJ* 1996; **312:** 1494-5.

[21] Avorn J, Soumerai SB. A new approach to reducing suboptimal drug use. *JAMA* 1983; **250:** 1728-32.

[22] Ray WA. Reducing antipsychotic drug prescribing for nursing-home patients: a controlled trial of the effect of an educational visit. *Am J Public Health* 1987; **77:** 1448-50.

[23] Mittman BS, Tonesk X, Jacobson PD. Implementing clinical practice guidelines: social influence strategies and practitioner behaviour change. *Quality Review Bulletin* 1992; December: 413-22.

[24] Barnes RD, Bell S. Interpractice visits by general practitioners. *Aust Fam Physician* 1994; **23:** 1922-8.

[25] Lomas J, Enkin M., Anderson GM, *et al.* Opinion leaders vs audit and feedback to implement practice guidelines: delivery after previous cesarean section. *JAMA* 1991; **265:** 2202-7.

[26] Oxman A, Davis D, Haynes RB, *et al.* No magic bullets: a systematic review of 102 trials of interventions to help health professionals deliver services more effectively or efficiently. *Can Med Assoc J* 1995; **153:** 1423-43.

[27] Johnston ME, Langton KB, Haynes RB, *et al.* The effects of computer based clinical decision support systems on clinical performance and patients' outcome. A critical appraisal of research. *Ann Intern Med* 1994; **120:** 135-42.

[28] Universities of Leeds and York. *Effective health care bulletins.* Edinburgh: Churchill Livingstone, 1996: **2:** 8; Leeds: Universities of Leeds and York. (Nuffield Institute for Health, 71-75 Clarendon Rd, Leeds LS2 9PL.)

[29] NCT/King's Fund. *Through the Maze: a comprehensive guide to sources of research-based information on pregnancy, birth and post-natal care.* London: National Childbirth Trust and the King's Fund, 1995. (Obtainable from the National Childbirth Trust, Maternity Sales, 239 Shawbridge Street, Glasgow G43 1QN.)

[30] British Diabetic Association. *Diabetes care: what you should expect.* London: British Diabetic Association, 1996. (Obtainable from British Diabetic Association, 10 Queen Anne St. London WC1.)

[31] Kasper J, Mulley A, Wennberg J. Developing shared decision-making programmes to improve the quality of health care. *Qual Rev Bull* 1992; **18**: 182-90.

[32] Coiera E. The Internet's challenge to health care provision. *BMJ* 1996; **312**: 3-4.

[33] Hurwitz B, Goodman C, Yudkin J. Prompting the care of non-insulin dependent (type II) diabetic patients in an inner city area: one model of community care. *BMJ* 1993; **306**: 624-30.

[34] Fulford KWM, Ersser S, Hope T. *Essential practice in patient-centred care.* Oxford: Blackwell Service, 1996.

[35] Rosenfeld R, Servo JC. Facilitating innovation in large organisations. In: West MA, Farr JL, eds. *Innovation and creativity at work.* Chichester: John Wiley, 1990.

[36] Schoenbaum SC, Gottlieb LK. Algorithm based improvement of clinical quality. *BMJ* 1990; **301**: 1374-6.

[37] Dunning M, McQuay H, Milne R. Getting a GRiPP. *Health Service Journal* 1994; **104**: 18-20.

[38] Appleby J, Walshe K, Ham C. *Acting on the evidence: a review of clinical effectiveness: sources of information, dissemination and implementation.* Birmingham: National Association of Health Authorities and Trusts, 1995.

[39] Department of Health. *Research for health.* London: HMSO, 1993.

[40] Research and Development Task Force. *Supporting research and development in the NHS.* London: HMSO, 1994. (Culyer report.)

[41] Advisory group to the NHS Central Research and Development Committee. *An agenda for the evaluation of methods to promote the implementation of research findings in the NHS.* Leeds: Department of Health, 1995.

# Appendix A: Checklists for finding, appraising, and implementing evidence

Unless otherwise stated, these checklists can be applied to randomised controlled trials, other controlled clinical trials, cohort studies, case-control studies, or any other research evidence.

## Is my practice evidence based?—a context-sensitive checklist for individual clinical encounters (see chapter 1)

1 Have I identified and prioritised the clinical, psychological, social, and other problem(s), taking into account the patient's perspective?

2 Have I performed a sufficiently competent and complete examination to establish the likelihood of competing diagnoses?

3 Have I considered additional problems and risk factors that may need opportunistic attention?

4 Have I, when necessary, sought evidence (from systematic reviews, guidelines, clinical trials, and other sources) pertaining to the problems?

5 Have I assessed and taken into account the completeness, quality, and strength of the evidence?

6 Have I applied valid and relevant evidence to this particular set of problems in a way that is both scientifically justified and intuitively sensible?

7 Have I presented the pros and cons of different options to the patient in a way they can understand and incorporated the patient's utilities into the final recommendation?

8 Have I arranged review, recall, referral, or other further care as necessary?

# Checklist for searching Medline or the Cochrane library (see chapter 2)

1 To look for an article you know exists, search by textwords (in title, abstract, or both) or use field suffixes for author, title, institution, journal, and publication year.

2 For a maximally sensitive search on a subject, search under both MeSH headings (exploded) and textwords (title and abstract), then combine the two by using the Boolean operator "or".

3 For a focused (specific) search on a clear cut topic, perform two or more sensitive searches as in (2), and combine them by using the Boolean operator "and".

4 To find articles that are likely to be of high methodological quality, insert an evidence based quality filter for therapeutic interventions, aetiology, diagnostic procedures, or epidemiology (see appendix B) and/or use maximally sensitive search strategies for randomised trials, systematic reviews, and meta-analyses (see appendix C).

5 Refine your search as you go along—for example, to exclude irrelevant material, use the Boolean operator "not".

6 Use subheadings only when this is the only practicable way of limiting your search as manual indexers are fallible and misclassifications are common.

7 When limiting a large set, browse through the last 50 or so abstracts yourself rather than expecting the software to pick the best half dozen.

# Checklist to determine what a paper is about (see chapter 3)

1 Why was the study done (what clinical question did it examine)?

2 What type of study was done?

- Primary research (experiment, randomised controlled trial, other controlled clinical trial, cohort study, case-control study, cross sectional survey, longitudinal survey, case report, or case series)?

- Secondary research (simple overview, systematic review, meta-analysis, decision analysis, guideline development, economic analysis)?

3  Was the study design appropriate to the broad field of research examined (therapy, diagnosis, screening, prognosis, causation)?

4  Was the study ethical?

## Checklist for the methods section of a paper (see chapter 4)

1  Was the study original?

2  Whom is the study about?

- How were subjects recruited?

- Who was included in and who was excluded from the study?

- Were the subjects studied in "real life" circumstances?

3  Was the design of the study sensible?

- What intervention or other manoeuvre was being considered?

- What outcome(s) were measured and how?

4  Was the study adequately controlled?

- If a "randomised trial" was randomisation truly random?

- If a cohort, case-control, or other non-randomised comparative study were the controls appropriate?

- Were the groups comparable in all important aspects except for the variable being studied?

- Was assessment of outcome (or, in a case-control study, allocation of caseness) "blind"?

5  Was the study large enough and continued for long enough, and was follow up complete enough, to make the results credible?

## Checklist for the statistical aspects of a paper (see chapter 5)

1  Have the authors set the scene correctly?

- Have they determined whether their groups are comparable and, if necessary, adjusted for baseline differences?

- What sort of data have they got and have they used appropriate statistical tests?

- If the statistical tests in the paper are obscure why have the authors chosen to use them?

- Have the data been analysed according to the original study protocol?

2  Paired data, tails, and outliers:

- Were paired tests performed on paired data?

- Was a two tailed test performed whenever the effect of an intervention could conceivably be a negative one?

- Were outliers analysed with both common sense and appropriate statistical adjustments?

3  Correlation, regression and causation:

- Has correlation been distinguished from regression and has the correlation coefficient ($r$ value) been calculated and interpreted correctly?

- Have assumptions been made about the nature and direction of causality?

4  Probability and confidence:

- Have P values been calculated and interpreted appropriately?

- Have confidence intervals been calculated and do the authors' conclusions reflect them?

5   Have the authors expressed their results in terms of the likely harm or benefit that an individual patient can expect, such as:

● Relative risk reduction

● Absolute risk reduction

● Number needed to treat

● Odds ratio.

## Checklist for material provided by a pharmaceutical company representative (see chapter 6)

1   Does this material cover a subject that interests me and is clinically important in my practice?

2   Has this material been published in independent peer reviewed journals? Has any significant evidence been omitted from this presentation or withheld from publication?

3   Does the material include high level evidence such as systematic reviews, meta-analyses, or double blind randomised controlled trials against the drug's closest competitor given at optimal dosage?

4   Have the trials or reviews examined a clearly focused, important and answerable clinical question that reflects a problem of relevance to patients? Do they provide evidence on safety, tolerability, efficacy, and price?

5   Has each trial or meta-analysis defined the condition to be treated, the patients to be included, the interventions to be compared, and the outcomes to be examined?

6   Does the material provide direct evidence that the drug will help my patients live a longer, healthier, more productive, or symptom free life?

7   If a surrogate outcome measure has been used, what is the evidence that it is reliable, reproducible, sensitive, specific, a true predictor of disease, and rapidly reflects the response to therapy?

181

8 Do trial results indicate whether (and how) the effectiveness of the treatments differed and whether there was a difference in the type or incidence of adverse reactions? Are the results expressed in terms of numbers needed to treat, and are they clinically as well as statistically significant?

9 If large amounts of material have been provided by the representative, which three papers provide the strongest evidence for the company's claims?

## Checklist for a paper that claims to validate a diagnostic or screening test (see chapter 7)

1 Is this test potentially relevant to my practice?

2 Has the test been compared with a true gold standard?

3 Did this validation study include an appropriate spectrum of subjects?

4 Has work up bias been avoided?

5 Has observer bias been avoided?

6 Was the test shown to be reproducible both within and between observers?

7 What are the features of the test as derived from this validation study?

8 Were confidence intervals given for sensitivity, specificity, and other features of the test?

9 Has a sensible "normal range" been derived from these results?

10 Has this test been placed in the context of other potential tests in the diagnostic sequence for the condition?

## Checklist for a systematic review or meta-analysis (see chapter 8)

1 Did the review examine an important clinical question?

2 Was a thorough search done of the appropriate database(s) and were other potentially important sources explored?

3 Was methodoligical quality assessed and the trials weighted accordingly?

4 How sensitive are the results to the way the review has been done?

5 Have the numerical results been interpreted with common sense and due regard to the broader aspects of the problem?

## Checklist for a set of clinical guidelines (see chapter 9)

1 Did the preparation and publication of these guidelines involve a significant conflict of interest?

2 Are the guidelines concerned with an appropriate topic, and do they state clearly the goal of ideal treatment in terms of health and/or cost outcome?

3 Was the guideline development panel headed by a leading expert in the field (ideally it should not be) and was a specialist in the methodology of secondary research (for example, meta-analyst, health economist) involved?

4 Have all the relevant data been scrutinised and do the guidelines' conclusions seem to be in keeping with the data?

5 Do they cover variations in medical practice and other controversial areas (for example, optimum care in response to genuine or perceived underfunding)?

6 Are the guidelines valid and reliable?

7 Are they clinically relevant, comprehensive, and flexible?

8 Do they take into account what is acceptable to, affordable by, and practically possible for patients?

9 Do they include recommendations for their own dissemination, implementation, and periodic review?

## Checklist for an economic analysis (see chapter 10)

1 Is the analysis based on a study that answers a clearly defined clinical question about an economically important issue?

2 Whose viewpoint are costs and benefits considered from?

3 Have the interventions being compared been shown to be clinically effective?

4 Are the interventions sensible and workable in the settings where they are likely to be applied?

5 Which method of economic analysis was used and was this appropriate?

- If the interventions produced identical outcomes ⇨ cost-minimisation analysis

- If the important outcome is unidimensional ⇨ cost-effectiveness analysis

- If the important outcome is multidimensional ⇨ cost-utility analysis

- If the cost-benefit equation for this condition needs to be compared with cost-benefit equations for different conditions ⇨ cost-benefit analysis

- If a cost-benefit analysis would otherwise be appropriate but the preference values given to different health states are disputed or likely to change ⇨ cost-consequences analysis.

6 How were costs and benefits measured?

7 Were incremental rather than absolute benefits compared?

8 Was health status in the "here and now" given precedence over health status in the distant future?

9 Was sensitivity analysis performed?

10 Were "bottom line" aggregate scores overused?

## Checklist for a qualitative research paper (see chapter 11)

1 Did the article describe an important clinical problem examined via a clearly formulated question?

2 Was the qualitative approach appropriate?

3 How were the setting and the subjects selected?

4 What was the researcher's perspective and has this been taken into account?

5 What methods did the researcher use for collecting data—and are these described in enough detail?

6 What methods did the researcher use to analyse the data—and what quality control measures were implemented?

7 Are the results credible and if so are they clinically important?

8 What conclusions were drawn and are they justified by the results?

9 Are the findings of the study transferable to other clinical settings?

## Checklist for health care organisations working towards an evidence based culture for clinical and purchasing decisions (see chapter 12 and refernce 38 of that chapter)

1 *Leadership*—How often has information on effectiveness or evidence based medicine been discussed at board meetings in the past 12 months? Has the board taken time out to learn about developments in clinical and cost effectiveness?

2 *Investment*—What resources are the organisation investing in finding and using clinical effectiveness information? Is there a planned approach to promoting evidence based medicine that is properly resourced and staffed?

3 *Using available resources*—What action has been taken by the organisation in response to EL(93)115 (Improving Clinical Effectiveness) and EL(94)74 (Improving the Effectiveness of the NHS)? What has changed in the organisation as a result?

4 *Implementation*—Who is responsible for receiving, acting on, and monitoring the implementation of Effective Health Care bulletins? What action has been taken on each of the bulletins issued to date?

5 *Clinical guidelines*—Who is responsible for receiving, acting on, and monitoring clinical practice guidelines? Do those arrangements ensure that both managers and clinicians play their part in guideline development and implementation?

6 *Training*—Has any training been provided to staff within the organisation (both clinical and non-clinical) on appraising and using evidence of effectiveness to influence clinical practice?

7 *Contracts*—How often does clinical and cost-effectiveness information form an important part of contract negotiation and agreement? How many contracts contain terms that set out how effectiveness information is to be used?

8 *Incentives*—What incentives—both individual and organisational—exist to encourage the practice of evidence based medicine? What disincentives exist to discourage inappropriate practice and unjustified variations in clinical decision making?

9 *Information systems*—Is the potential of existing information systems to monitor clinical effectiveness being used to the full? Is there a business case for new information systems to deal with the task, and is this issue being considered when purchasing decisions about information technology are made?

10 *Clinical audit*—Is there an effective clinical audit programme throughout the organisation, capable of examining issues of clinical effectiveness and bringing about appropriate changes in practice?

# Appendix B: Evidence based quality filters for everyday use

1 Therapeutic interventions (What works?)

1 exp clinical trials

2 exp research design

3 randomised controlled trial.pt

4 clinical trial.pt

5 (single or double or treble or triple).tw

6 (mask$ or blind$).tw

7 5 and 6

8 placebos / or placebo.tw

9 1 or 2 or 3 or 4 or 7 or 8

2 Aetiology (What causes it? What are the risk factors?)

1 exp causality

2 exp cohort studies

3 exp risk

4 1 or 2 or 3

## 3 Diagnostic procedures

1   exp "sensitivity and specificity"

2   exp diagnostic errors

3   exp mass screening

4   1 or 2 or 3

## 4 Epidemiology

1   sn.xs

(this would find all articles indexed under any MeSH term with any of "statistics", "epidemiology", "ethnology", or "mortality" as subheadings)

# Appendix C: Maximally sensitive search strings (to be used mainly for research)

1 Maximally sensitive qualifying string for randomised controlled trials

1 RANDOMISED CONTROLLED TRIAL.pt
2 CONTROLLED CLINICAL TRIAL.pt
3 RANDOMISED CONTROLLED TRIALS.sh
4 RANDOM ALLOCATION.sh
5 DOUBLE-BLIND METHOD.sh
6 SINGLE-BLIND METHOD.sh
7 or/1-6
8 ANIMALS.sh. not HUMAN.sh
9 7 not 8
10 CLINICAL TRIAL.pt
11 exp CLINICAL TRIALS
12 (clin$ adj25 trial$).ti,ab
13 ((single or double or treble or triple) adj25 (blind$ or mask$)).ti,ab
14 PLACEBOS.sh
15 placebo$.ti,ab
16 random$.ti,ab
17 RESEARCH DESIGN.sh
18 or/10-17
19 18 not 8

20  19 not 9

21  COMPARATIVE STUDY.sh

22  exp EVALUATION STUDIES/

23  FOLLOW UP STUDIES.sh

24  PROSPECTIVE STUDIES.sh

25  (control$ or prospectiv$ or volunteer$).ti,ab

26  or/21-25

27  26 not 8

28  27 (not 9 or 20)

29  9 or 20 or 28

(In these examples, upper case denotes controlled vocabulary and lower case denotes free text terms. Search statements 8, 9, 19, and 27 could be omitted if your search seems to be taking an unacceptably long time to run.)

## 2  Maximally sensitive qualifying string for identifying systematic reviews

1  REVIEW, ACADEMIC.pt

2  REVIEW, TUTORIAL.pt

3  META-ANALYSIS.pt

4  META-ANALYSIS.sh

5  systematic$ adj25 review$

6  systematic$ adj25 overview$

7  meta-analy$ or metaanaly$ or (meta analy$)

8  or/1-7

9  ANIMAL.sh. not HUMAN.sh

10  8 not 9

(Search statements 9 and 10 could be omitted if your search seems to be taking an unacceptably long time to run.)

# Appendix D: Assessing the effects of an intervention

| Group | Outcome event | | Total |
| --- | --- | --- | --- |
| | Yes | No | |
| Control group | a | b | a + b |
| Experimental group | c | d | c + d |

Control event rate = risk of outcome event in control group =
CER = a/(a+b)

Experimental event rate = risk of outcome event in experimental
group = EER = c/(c+d)

Relative risk reduction (RRR) = (CER-EER)/CER

Absolute risk reduction (ARR) = CER-EER

Number needed to treat (NNT) = 1/ARR = 1/(CER-EER)

Odds ratio =
$$\frac{\text{(odds of outcome event } vs \text{ odds of no event) in experimental group}}{\text{(odds of outcome event } vs \text{ odds of no event) in control group}}$$

(The outcome event can be desirable (for example, cure) or
undesirable (for example, an adverse drug reaction). In the latter
case, it is semantically preferable to refer to numbers needed to
harm and to the relative or absolute risk *increase*.)

# Index

1. What is it    300 w                    10
2. Personal EBHC roles    300–400    20
3. Desire Skills of EBHC.   300–400    20
4. Self ass't of EBHC skills 300–5
5. How demonstrate abilities 300    10
6. Which ones you choosen    300    10

# EBM Skills List

1. Not to get overwhelmed by the variety of sources available.

## Needs

1. To understand different parts of Cochrane.